EXECUTIVE EXCELLENCE

PROTOCOLS *for*
Healthcare Leaders
Second Edition

D1503080

American College of Healthcare Executives
Management Series Editorial Board

Chip Caldwell, FACHE
Institute for Interactive Accelerated Change

Virginia V. Cohen, FACHE
Center for Quality Innovations and Research

Terence T. Cunningham, FACHE
The Johns Hopkins Hospital

Mark A. Dame, CHE
Jackson Memorial Hospital

Kenneth C. DeBoer
Avera St. Luke's

John Di Perry, Jr., CHE
Mercy Medical Center

William L. Dowling, PH.D. (FA)
University of Washington

Michael R. Gloor, FACHE
St. Francis Medical Center

Bob J. Haley, FACHE
Columbia Medical Center of Denton

Bruce A. Harma, CHE
tricare Management Activity

Karolee M. Sowle, FACHE
Desert Regional Medical Center

Katherine W. Vestal, PH.D., FACHE
Ernst & Young LLP

EXECUTIVE EXCELLENCE

PROTOCOLS *for* Healthcare Leaders
Second Edition

Carson F. Dye

Health Administration Press
ACHE Management Series

Your board, staff, or clients may also benefit from this book's insight. For more information on quantity discounts, contact the Health Administration Press Marketing Manager at (312) 424-9470.

Copyright © 2000 by the Foundation of the American College of Healthcare Executives. Printed in the United States of America. All rights reserved. This book or parts thereof may not be reproduced in any form without written permission of the publisher. Opinions and views expressed in this book are those of the author and do not necessarily reflect those of the Foundation of the American College of Healthcare Executives.

04   03   02   01   00   5   4   3   2   1

Library of Congress Cataloging-in-Publication Data

Dye, Carson F.
    Executive Excellence: protocols for healthcare leaders/Carson F. Dye.—2nd ed.
        p.   cm. — (ACHE management series)
    Rev. ed. of: Protocols for health care executive behavior, c1993.
    Includes bibliographical references.
    ISBN 1-56793-142-1 (alk. paper)
        1. Health services administrators—Conduct of life. 2. Business etiquette. I. Dye, Carson F. Protocols for health care executive behavior II. Title. III. Management series (Ann Arbor, Mich.)
        [DNLM: 1. Health Services Administration. 2. Administrative Personnel. 3. Ethics, Professional. 4. Interpersonal Relations. 5. Leadership. W 84.1 D995e 2000]
        RA971.D937 2000
        362. 1'068'4—dc21   00-058203
                                                                        CIP

The paper used in this publication meets the minimum requirements of American National Standards for Information Sciences—Permanence of Paper for Printed Library Materials, ANSI Z39.48–1984. ∞ ™

Health Administration Press
A division of the Foundation of the
    American College of Healthcare Executives
One North Franklin Street, Suite 1700
Chicago, IL 60606-3491
312/424-2800

To those who have gone before me—
    for their examples, both good and bad;
To those who will take the next steps—
    their service and accomplishments yet
    to be fulfilled;
To those who teach;
To those whose strong values guide them; and
To my family, who allow me freedom and
    show me great love.
I thank all.

CONTENTS

Acknowledgments

I have been so blessed in my career. I have worked in several magnificent healthcare organizations and have had the advantage of working with some of the finest leaders in healthcare. Over the past ten years, I have had the privilege to consult for and counsel several very strong client organizations and work with their superb leaders. From these wonderful leaders I observed and learned many principles of protocols. This book is the product of those observations as well as many other experiences. These leaders showed me, often unknowingly, that right and wrong indeed exist in even the grayest of issues; their examples pointed to the appropriateness of behavior. I thank them for their examples and values.

As an author, I am faced with the task of listing names of individuals whose values and behavior helped inspire this book. For those whom I do not list, I hope you do not take offense because your exclusion is unintended. My special thanks go to the following very special leaders who have that keen sense of the appropriate: Mark Hannahan, Michael Gilligan, James Kaskie, Bob Sholis, Bob Coons, David Purcell, Kam Sigafoos, Ed Cotter, Sy Sokatch, the late Dr. Lonnie Wright, Mike Keeney, Tom Ruthemeyer, Ed Curtis, Otis Wilson, Paul Nurick, Susan Hunsaker, Sister Nancy Linenkugel, Bill Ruse, Carol Cogossi, Walter McLarty, Keith Allen, Brad Need, Bill Kessler, Randy

Oostra, Steve Mickus, and Dr. Lee Hammerling. These, and other, leaders have either directly discussed behavioral protocols with me or have shown me through examples that appropriate behavior may be the most important factor in success. I also want to acknowledge the late Dr. Ed Arlinghouse, the former chair of the graduate program at Xavier University, who helped sow the seeds of this book over twenty years ago by presenting his three-factor model of success to me—then a young executive. Also, I have gained greatly from my association with Dr. Jared Lock of Hogan Assessment Systems.

I am also appreciative of the many individuals who have participated in the many workshops I have taught over the past twenty years. I have learned so much from them and their interactions. Particular appreciation also goes to those who taught with me including Dr. Greg Taylor, Dr. Ed Pike, Steve Strasser, and Steve Mickus. Also, I have greatly benefited from my close association with Dick Rand of The Healthcare Roundtable.

Average books gain life under the direction of great editors. My editor, Jane Williams at Health Administration Press, is simply superb. She made this work more enjoyable and also greatly improved its organization and message. I also wish to recognize Rob Fromberg, also at Health Administration Press, for his continuing support. We in the healthcare industry should be proud of the contributions of Health Administration Press and its staff. Our small industry benefits greatly from the work they produce.

And last but not least: I have learned that in life nothing is more sacred or important than family. Mine is the greatest and I acknowledge and express respect for my four magnificent daughters—Carly, Emily, Liesl, and Blakely. All are different young women, and all do much to inspire me. Special mention of my wife and partner, Joaquina, is very appropriate and deserved here. She has been a great support for many years, and she continuously serves so many positive roles in my work and life. These five women are a wonderful and loving support system for this road warrior.

Foreword

by Rush Jordan

All of us are indebted to Carson Dye for this second edition of *Executive Excellence: Protocols for Healthcare Executives.* One painful lesson we learn in management is that the higher we progress in the organization the less feedback we receive from peers and subordinates. Senior executives frequently become isolated and overlook the fact that the unwritten rules of management excellence can make or break their careers. Thus, astute executives seek out a coach from a like organization or a consultant to help guide their behavior, on the job and off the job.

This book can serve as an ethical, insightful coach for executives at all levels in the organization. Establishing a reputation for integrity begins with your first day on the job. The more-concise edition is reduced in length, better organized, and updated to meet the needs of healthcare executives in the 21st century. Three new chapters add great value to this book: "Governing Board," "Physician Relationships," and "Cultural and Gender Diversity." In my opinion, these chapters are required reading.

Unfortunately, protocols for executive excellence are not taught in the majority of our graduate programs. This book should be the basis for a course to better prepare our graduates for the real world. Rarely do we find those protocols listed in a symposium brochure, with the possible exception of the brochures of the American College of Healthcare Executives. The concerned CEO would be wise to include these topics in his or her organization's management-development seminars.

These are turbulent times in the healthcare industry. Even the most successful or most confident executive would greatly enhance his or her future by reading *Executive Excellence* to complete a "check-up" on behaviors inside and outside the organizational setting.

L. R. (Rush) Jordan, LFACHE
President-Emeritus
Miami Valley Hospital
Dayton, Ohio
and
Professor
University of Alabama at Birmingham

Preface

Leadership in a world of dilemmas is not, fundamentally, a matter of style, charisma, or professional management technique. It is a difficult daily quest for integrity. Managers' behavior should be an unadorned, consistent reflection of what they believe and what they aspire to for a company.

Joseph L. Badaracco, Jr., and Richard R. Ellsworth in
Leadership and the Quest for Integrity (1993)

Scenario 1: A director of a leading health administration program received a phone call from one of the program's former "star" students. Aside from catching up with his former advisor, the student also had some distressing news: He has just been given six months to leave his post as an assistant administrator at a hospital. The student continued to say that his release was a complete surprise because he was recently tapped for a promotion. Further probing by the director revealed that a week ago the student attended a medical staff party hosted by the medical staff president at his home. In the party, the student drank too much; incessantly made obnoxious remarks about the home, the party, the staff, and the hospital; and told offensive jokes. A few days later, the student's boss informed him that his behavior at the party greatly embarrassed and appalled the medical staff president and his wife, many physicians, and other attendees. The boss also expressed his dismay and warned the student that because of the incident, the student's credibility was now greatly diminished and his chances for continued success at the hospital was now nonexistent.

Scenario 2: A successful, well-liked, and unmarried CEO began dating the ex-wife of a former hospital board member. The ex-husband, and former board member, disapproved and was jealous of the relationship, so he led a personal and professional attack against the CEO to discredit and replace him. The ensuing controversy created a schism among the board and the medical staff members, which harmed staff morale, the quality of care, and the bottom line of the hospital for several years. In the midst of the conflict, the CEO left embittered and unable to reassert his authority, restore his image, and redirect the hospital.

Scenario 3: A vice president of professional services was twice overlooked for promotion to the COO position, despite having the skills and experience appropriate for the job. The reason he could not move forward was simple—he lacked the unequivocal confidence of the medical staff. Several members of the medical staff were aware that he had romantic relationships with several nurse managers, and they believed that these relationships—although in the past—could bias his judgment and hamper his ability and responsibility to decide fairly on organizational matters. Although the medical staff was comfortable with him as VP of professional services, they were against his appointment to a higher, more visible position.

The above scenarios exemplify only few of the hundreds of real-world dilemmas that not only fuel ethical discussions—and gossip—in classrooms, boardrooms, and lunchrooms but also, most importantly, dictate the professional fate of the "offending" healthcare executive. As an executive search consultant, I have witnessed and heard of cases, much similar to the three mentioned above, in which technically proficient careerists are professionally stunted, if not destroyed, because of seemingly minor inappropriate acts such as using office equipment, supplies, funds, and manpower for personal gain; getting romantically involved with subordinates; being verbally abusive to staff and colleagues; or developing annoying personal habits. As a former healthcare executive, I have interacted with other executives—new and experienced alike—who behave poorly and offensively not because of malicious intent, but simply because they lack a sense of the appropriate and are unaware of others' perception and the countless consequences of their conduct; only a few colleagues feel knowledgeable about or comfortable with offering constructive criticism. Further, many executives judge their professional success solely based on meeting organizational goals, such as increasing financial profitability or market share. What's missing in this evaluation of professional success is a mirror that would impartially reflect the executive's day-to-day interaction and effects on others, as well as on her/himself.

THE EXECUTIVE EXCELLENCE EQUATION

A successful organization is characterized by a consistently strong bottom line; a high degree of quality patient care; a charitable and pioneering reputation; an innovative and technologically advanced treatment capability; a highly competent, caring, and loyal staff; and a substantial market share. Assuming that a successful organization is the product of its successful leaders, then what characterizes these leaders? A successful leader possesses competency in four areas:

1. Technical: specialized knowledge such as budgeting, accounting, etc.
2. Administrative: organizational skill such as scheduling, prioritizing, etc.
3. Human Resources: managerial ability such as interacting with employees, resolving conflict, etc.

Figure PI: The Executive Excellence Equation

Technical skills
+ *Administrative* skills
+ *Human resources* skills
+ understanding of *Protocols* (behavioral)

= **Executive Excellence**

---

4. Protocols (behavioral): personal understanding of rules of proper conduct and its effects on self and others such as being respectful, showing courtesy, etc.

Competence in four interrelated factors contributes to executive excellence. Some executives believe that expertise in the first factor of the equation is enough because it is the most measurable and predictable. But this school of thought only produces leaders who, although knowledgeable about their craft, are one-dimensional.

DEFINITIONS

TECHNICAL SKILL

Technical skill is the practical and in-depth knowledge of a specialized field. In healthcare, an executive's technical skill generally means:

- awareness of clinical quality and physician issues;
- comprehension of the legal nature of corporations and organizational structures;
- experience and competence in working with boards of trustees;
- knowledge of the importance and consequences of organizational publicity;

- ability to analyze and comprehend financial aspects of performance;
- proficiency in coordinating organizational activities;
- ability to assess the performance of the organizations and seek ways to improve quality; and
- comprehension of the overall role of the office and the general organizational structure.

Specific technical skills are often dictated by the executive's specialization. For example, financial executives, who are mostly certified public accountants (CPAs), have to be highly proficient in budgeting, accounting, investing, and assessing financial risks. Nursing executives have to fully understand nursing care plans, clinical pathways and maps, clinical quality measures, and requirements of the Joint Commission on Accreditation of Health Care Organizations (JCAHO). Human resources executives must know labor and employment law, benefits and compensation, and job-evaluation tools.

ADMINISTRATIVE SKILL

Administrative skills relate to office organization and management, which include:

- ability to forecast, budget, and develop monitoring mechanisms;
- competence in coordinating and scheduling activities;
- experience with running meetings; and
- knowledge of setting strategic planning objectives.

HUMAN RESOURCES SKILL

Human resources skill is the ability to take charge of work, workers, and work environment. The responsibilities, outside of the technical aspects, include:

- relating to individuals and groups of employees;
- delegating duties;
- creating and sustaining a positive, motivating environment;
- giving appraisal and feedback;
- resolving and controlling conflicts; and
- managing stress.

UNDERSTANDING PROTOCOLS

Although certainly an important factor in executive excellence, the subject of protocols is seldom addressed in graduate school courses, textbooks, or managerial seminars. However, following protocols is a crucial requirement during periods of organizational stress and crisis.

The Fourth Factor in the Equation

In healthcare, the term protocol typically refers to proper medical procedure or commonly accepted way of doing things to and for the patients. Many medical protocols are not written in any codified manner; they are frequently passed on from one generation of physicians to another, often during medical rounds. Another type of protocols is behavioral. Although the phrase behavioral protocols connotes a certain rigidity in speech and action—that "stiff upper lip" notion that hides our true feelings and opinions—its ultimate purpose is actually engaging: to guide leaders in adopting and practicing a set of rules that would protect them and others from potentially irreversible and professionally damaging situations. Because no single standard can cover every possible situation that executives encounter, no general code of conduct currently exists that governs all of the various behavioral expectations of organizations. Therefore, healthcare executives must subscribe to what the majority of the public sees as "socially acceptable" or "right" and "wrong." For successful executives, this socially prescribed behavior is second nature because they practice it everyday with each interaction and it has become part of their characteristics. These leaders are poised, sensitive to others' perceptions, and always willing to modify their conduct to fit any given situation. This is not to say, however, that all successful executives behave accordingly. In fact, successful executives who have annoying and offending habits and who do not realize the consequences of their actions do exist. However, they are rare partly because healthcare organizations simply would not tolerate the abuse and eventually terminate them. The major difference between these two groups of successful leaders is one group is aware that personal eccentricities can be curbed and good conduct can be learned and practiced.

As discussed in my book, *Leadership in Healthcare*, the higher the executive moves up the organizational ladder, the more intimidated her/his subordinates become and the less likely the chances that she/he will receive constructive and direct criticism on her/his behavior, not even from colleagues. A probable cause for this lack of advice is that colleagues and subordinates fear that the executive may misconstrue their suggestion to signal a personality clash or difference in philosophy or approach. Most feedback relates only to the executive's organizational decisions or input because these factors are quantifiable and not subjective as personal conduct. As a result, some executives fail to see the behaviors that eventually cost them their careers.

Executives must observe proper protocols every minute of everyday not only to salvage their image but to smoothen their daily encounters within the organization, especially because they are always being observed by others—from subordinates to board members. Figure PII is a litany of real complaints from actual healthcare employees confessed to me as a search consultant.

Notice that none of the negative statements in Figure PII talked about the executives lacking poor technical skills—no one complains about downsizing because of weak bottom line or low census and no one is concerned about the high turnover rate.

Figure PII: Common Complaints About Leaders

- From a board member to an executive search consultant who had been secretly called in to begin a search for a new CEO: "She gets results, but she is really turning off some of the key physicians with her abrasive personality and peculiar attributes. I think that we should begin to look for a new CEO."
- From a RN about the COO: "Why didn't she speak to me? She really seems to ignore me when she walks through the hall."
- From the majority of executive team members about their CEO: "I just don't feel comfortable around him. It is impossible to know what he's thinking and he's really difficult to read."
- From several assistant administrators about a CFO: "He's a great man to work for as long as you agree with him."
- From most of the employees about their administrator in a religious organization: "I've never seen a person whose mood can affect an organization so much."
- From a senior executive about a CEO who has extreme mood shifts: "He is just not consistent. If he were, he would be a better leader."

The functional value of appropriate behavior of the executives mentioned in Figure PII has approached zero. Understanding and following behavioral protocols add to the value of an executive, so a zero value in that factor reduces the total value in the executive excellence equation.

CHAPTER OVERVIEW

Chapters 1, 2, and 3—Perception Versus Reality, Professional Image, and Professional Reputation—explore various misconceptions that result in distrust and schism not only between executives and staff, but also among organizational leaders. These chapters call out the negative effects of status symbols associated with prestigious leadership posts, enumerate dos and don'ts of internal and external conduct, and prescribe ways of strengthening influence by adhering to the basic concepts of respect.

Chapter 4—Ethical Decisions—reiterates the importance of following a code of ethics in personal and professional growth. Chapter 5—Interpersonal Relationships—correlates selfless and humble interaction with staff and subordinate managers to obtaining desired outcomes.

Chapter 6—The Work Force—argues that executives, if they only dedicate the time to do so, and the rank and file have a lot more in common than what either party admits to. This chapter, which is an offshoot to Chapter 5, submits that executives should actually "abandon the open door policy" to become closer to their employees. Chapter 7—Executive Team Members—agrees that teamwork inevitably breeds jealousy, envy, and tunnel vision. However, the chapter submits protocols, including tips on fighting fair, that can cure these ills. Chapter 8—Governing Board—details the responsibilities, roles, and contribution of each board member to encourage executives to get involved in board-member selection process and to improve their relationship with members. Chapter 9—Human Resources—urges executives to consider ethical ramifications of human resources decisions, particularly employee termination. The chapter also discusses concepts such as developing a due process system and a human resources philosophy. Chapter 10—Written and Verbal Communication—emphasizes the importance of verbal and nonverbal communication in establishing relationship and strengthening credibility.

Chapter 11—Physician Relationships—acknowledges the widely known, but tacit, animosity between executives and physicians. The protocols in this chapter intend to enhance the executive's understanding of physician behavior. Chapter 12—Recruitment and Selection—contends that staff turnover is an ongoing war in the healthcare industry, but catalogs protocols that will help executives win at least some of the battles. Chapter 13—The New Position—presents basic protocols for executives who are new in the organization or just starting a new position. Chapter 14—The Office—posits that the office must reflect the executive's professional standards so its occupants must ensure the appropriateness of the physical space and must adhere to proper conduct outside of the office. The chapter addresses issues that are often taken for granted including office decorations; treatment of office mates, particularly the support staff; and personal conduct at social functions. Chapter 15—Cultural and Gender Diversity—is a comprehensive study of the changing faces of healthcare. The chapter includes statistical information and submits protocols that promote and support increasing diversity in the workplace and the boardroom.

The Epilogue and Appendix present tools that the executive can use to enhance her/his understanding of the protocols throughout.

GOALS

Executive Excellence is the culmination of my interest in and passion for the subject of executive behavior; an interest sparked by what I have observed during my almost thirty-year career in healthcare administration. As I have done in the first edition of this book, I still contend that graduate programs do not emphasize appropriate behavior enough in their teachings and that very few professional seminars offer courses about the topic. Although skill-development workshops on topics such as financial management, clinical care management, strategic planning, and marketing provide executives the technical insight needed to perform their primary duties, they do not cover the equally important interpersonal factors. Similarly, although books on personal and business etiquette and countless management skills literature are available, and generally helpful, they are not geared specifically to address the ethical dilemmas of healthcare executives and organizations. These are the reasons that I decided to revise the first edition of this book.

This book intends to serve two purposes: (1) to replicate — as a mirror does — images of real executive behaviors in real health-care settings and situations; and (2) to offer guidance — as constructive criticism should — on the unwritten rules, or gray areas, of behavior that govern what, who, where, when, why, and how we as executives say and do anything. These rules are called protocols. How we abide by them determines our personal and professional excellence or mediocrity.

Carson F. Dye, FACHE

Chapter One

PERCEPTION VERSUS REALITY

Bosses—especially senior ones—overestimate the significance of their routine decision-making and underestimate the
impact of their personal behavior.

Walter F. Ulmer, Jr., in *Center for
Creative Leadership* Newsletter

MANAGEMENT IS THE process of engineering the
perceptions of other people and maintaining it to better reflect reality. This maxim is as true now as it was
in 1993, when the first edition of this book was published. What
also remains true is the distance between executives and their
staff. Despite the trend of a relaxed work atmosphere and the
emergence of assertive employees, executives remain forebod-
ing figures in the healthcare industry. Consequently, executives
are not often challenged by their employees and, worse, not
openly criticized nor offered suggestions for personal or professional improvement. Even when executives are challenged by
an outspoken employee, they will often retreat into the privacy
and comfort of their offices and delegate the duty of responding
to a lower-rank executive. This retreat protects them from the

1

realities of their organization, and their absence skews their perception of the needs of the organization, staff, and peers.

The distance between executives and employees only deepens the gap because (1) it creates two differing perceptions of reality and (2) employees misunderstand, and possibly get offended by, the executive's lack of insight into the issues within their organizations. The bottom line in this conflict is people believe what they perceive to be true, albeit all the valid evidence that proves otherwise. The responsibility of managing this perception belongs solely to the executive. Consider the following examples:

- A male CEO is labeled as sexist for proposing a new rule that prevents female employees from walking to the parking lot at night unescorted by security guards.
- A group of Asian nurses organizes a blue flu, or a sick out, to protest a rumored salary differential between them and Caucasian nurses.
- The entire staff of a department believes that executives only visit for superficial, public-relations reasons and are not genuinely concerned about the status of the unit and its employees.

These cases are similar because they all revolve around half-truths. To respond to and combat these situations, executives must respond to the charges and follow the protocols of conduct accordingly.

1. *Recognize the perception.* Pretending that a misunderstanding is not happening will not make it go away, so admit it without personalizing it and seek ways to remedy it.
2. *Find out the genesis of the perception.* Ask or research how the perceived issue was started, but do not veil your

---

Figure 1.1: Protocols of Conduct

Because implication does not equal inference, executives must ensure that everyone received the intended messages and meanings by:

1. Recognizing the perception;
2. Finding out the genesis of the perception;
3. Changing or correcting the perception; and
4. Maintaining good perception.

---

efforts or pit one employee against another by recruiting help because doing so would only multiply the wrong impression.

3. *Change or correct the perception.* The only way to address a conflict is to face it, so talk with people and offer an explanation or apology if needed. Handling the matter yourself is the quickest way to convince people that you are interested in what they think. Correcting the matter is the quickest way to convince people that you care.

4. *Maintain good perception.* Keeping your subordinates informed and invested in the truth will ensure that half-truths will not be as pervasive. Again, management involves manipulating frequently misunderstood and misinterpreted words and symbols.

Unfortunately, in reality, some executives do not practice any kind of protocols when managing employee perception. These executives do not follow up on issues raised by the rank and file as thoroughly because in their minds, accountability to subordinate employees decreases as their accountability to higher authority—CEOs and boards of trustees—increases, as the following set of actual cases illustrates.

3

Case 1: The CEO of a hospital prided himself on his ability to relate to all levels of employees. He would frequently tell the staff that he used to work in an emergency room and knew what things were like on the "front lines." He believed that he had a lot of credibility with the rank and file and could understand them better than most executives. He would frequently tell his administrative staff that he was a "man of the people."

In his sixth year at the hospital, a serious union-organizing drive was initiated. During the union campaign, the CEO spent a great deal of time touring the various work areas, talking with employees, and encouraging them to support the hospital by voting against the union. After he had toured the hospital to express his support for the anti-union, pro-hospital stance, several maintenance employees remarked to the VP of human resources that this visit to their work areas was the first any of them remembered. A number of the housekeeping and dietary employees also observed that the CEO seldom visited their areas.

Ultimately, the hospital won the election and kept the union out. The "man of the people" once again became busy in the executive suite and seldom ventured out to have any meaningful contact with rank-and-file employees.

Case 2: A hospital executive was very active in a number of local organizations and service clubs. He believed that his community service was providing excellent visibility for his organization. However, after his resignation the committee in charge of looking for his replacement told the executive search consultant that they wanted candidates who would spend more time on the job and less with the chamber of commerce, Rotary Club, and other activities.

Case 3: A popular executive who had held several offices within his organization was eventually selected president. The following year, he was pushed out of his position by the medical staff who made his tenure very difficult. The medical staff was convinced that he had not spent enough time at the organization and delegated too much authority and responsibility to his COO and CFO.

Case 4: A hospital CEO made weekly visits to the operating room beginning at 6:30 A.M. to make himself available to the surgeons. He did this because he thought doing so would enhance his communication with them and show that he was sensitive to their needs and concerns. However, two of the more vocal surgeons told him that they actually viewed his presence as an interruption and a delay. After hearing this, he stopped his early morning visits and met with them at more convenient times.

Another form of failing to manage employee perception is when executives take advantage of perquisites, or perqs, which are tangible representations of the value of the executive. These highly visible perqs, although desirable and almost expected for each high-paying position, could host a litany of true conflicts including:

- imbalance of power. Some employees in all levels feel inferior and disillusioned because they think they work harder, and possibly are more educated or trained, but do not receive enough compensation nor special treatment or consideration. This perception is a factor in insubordination, high turnover rate, and low employee morale.
- financial turmoil. Once several employees get infected with the wrong perception, spreading the same way of thinking to a larger group of employees is fast and easy. The immediate result of this spread is low productivity, and the long-term effect affects the bottom line.

Although I do not submit that these perqs be abolished, I do submit that being aware of how employees perceive these perqs should be a main priority for executives. The following perqs are especially prone to misinterpretation.

1. *Reserved parking spaces.* To most workers, a reserved parking space is the ultimate symbol of being "the boss". It is the one symbol of importance that is most envied, especially when finding a place to park is difficult, sometimes dangerous, and inconvenient for everyone else.
2. *Expensive cars.* Access to a company car, or funds to buy or lease one, is a benefit for some executives and a crux of dismay for many employees. Consider the following real-life examples: (1) A hospital CEO drove a new Porsche each year during the hospital's most financially strained time during which employees were being laid off and patient services were being cut to reduce cost. (2) Members of a senior management team all drove newly leased cars at a time when their organization was in a grave financial condition.
3. *Executive dining areas.* Some healthcare organizations reserve elaborate dining rooms for their physicians and executives, but subject the rest of the employees to eat in utilitarian cafes.
4. *Free, catered meals.* Although sensible and valid reasons for catered meals exist, such as private meetings with physicians, significant community leaders, board members, etc. Executives, especially those who have catered lunch or breakfast regularly, must carefully consider the necessity of having free meals delivered or ordered. Consider this real-life example: A vice president for human resources was having a celebratory lunch with an employee of the month. The employee remarked that free lunches must be a benefit that comes with management jobs and then asked how many times a week the vice president paid for his own lunch.

5. *Laundered shirts.* At one hospital, a private laundry service delivered laundered shirts to the executives. Although the executives paid the full price personally for this service, many employees perceived that the hospital was picking up the tab.

Although perception is not reality, it is what matters most to many employees. This perception applies to anything that executives do—where they park, how they speak to others, how they physically touch employees, or how they pay for their personal supplies, including postage and stationery.

Managing perception is not an easy task. Because it involves a lot of convincing through honest actions and words and very intelligent and highly sophisticated professionals, the task itself can be misconstrued. As always, the best first steps in managing anything is following appropriate protocols, some of which are enumerated below. Although they are general in nature, these protocols have specific applications to numerous areas of executive life.

Respect others. As many executives move up in their organizations, they do not realize that they start to grow less tolerant of others' views and backgrounds and show less respect. They start achieving success by promoting their ways to the exclusion of other viewpoints. The open exchange of ideas and acceptance of diversity, including cultural and racial diversity, become obsolete from their typical managerial style because their advancement has reinforced their personal views. Because many executives achieve their positions by being fiercely competitive and by winning at all costs, they become somewhat callous toward others. The protocol in this case is for executives to replace callousness with sensitivity and respect. Consider the following definition of leadership by author F. G. Bailey in his book *Humbuggery and Manipulation: The Art of Leadership*:

Leadership ... cannot be done in any honest, open, rea-
soned, dispassionate, and scientific fashion. The leader must
be partisan. He must use rhetoric. He must be ruthless, be
ready to subvert values while appearing to support them,
and be clever enough to move the discourse up to a level
where opportunism can be successfully hidden behind a
screen of sermonizing about the eternal verities. Leadership is a form of cultivating ignorance, of stopping doubts,
and stifling questions.

Although all executives occasionally yield to the mode of leadership prescribed by Bailey, adding his recommendation into an
executive's everyday managerial style is frightening because at
some point subordinates will see through such deceitfulness and
will turn immediately against their executives. Furthermore, subordinates who work under such autocratic conditions and pres-
sures likely become "yes" people, seldom give their full and true
opinions, or may hide facts that might cause their superiors personal or professional discomfort. As a result, executives may find
themselves making decisions without the benefit of thoroughly
examining all the facts surrounding the issues.

Showing respect for others does not mean that executives must
always capitulate to someone else's views or methods. It does
mean, however, that executives must give some consideration to
those who have a different approach and show some regard for
their beliefs and principles.

Executives who are building teams should note that strong
teams are not composed of people who think and act alike. The
strongest teams, whether in sports or in management, are composed of members who have different strengths and can play
different roles. Unfortunately, in American healthcare organizations, executives tend to build management teams by selecting
members on the basis of which graduate school they attended or
the kinds of organizations in which they have worked. For example, many executives of large hospitals do not believe that

executives of smaller hospitals have the ability to be successful in large organizations, and executives of teaching hospitals often choose staff only from other teaching hospitals. This "club" mentality makes developing true respect for others difficult. Although homogeneous groups that attended the same graduate schools or have worked at similar institutions may have some diversity, they often lack sufficient variety and versatility to develop group strength for optimal team effectiveness.

The past couple of decades have increased the American society's awareness and understanding of diverse views, practices, cultures, and ethnicities. Our society has pushed its participants toward accepting disparate philosophies and customs, an acceptance that is evident in the increasing cultural diversity of the work place. Part of showing respect for others is acknowledging, welcoming, and working with those who are different in age, gender, race, culture, education, and physical and mental abilities.

Communicate in "sound bites." Executives usually lead very busy lives. As executives advance in rank and responsibility, the number of activities for which they are accountable increases proportionately. As a result, they have less time to focus on issues and can afford only few face-to-face encounters with employees. This inattentiveness can become an issue with the rank and file. Department supervisors clearly spend much more time with their staff than do executives; in fact, many first-line supervisors spend the majority of the day with their staff. Because executives have limited time, they must spend it wisely and make up in quality what they cannot afford in quantity.

Executives should view all their communication as politician's sound bites during a political campaign because, unlike lower-level executives, they have only a few moments to make a lasting, favorable impression. The "sound bite" concept is not only applicable when talking with employees, but also when communicating with individuals outside the office. For example, because executives are the most visible representation of an organization, their statements at civic club meetings or in social situations often are interpreted as *the* organization's official stance, so they should carefully monitor what they say at these outings. The following suggestions can improve executive sound bites.

1. *Be careful with casual comments.* Executives should carefully calculate the impact of comments they make to employees during their brief encounters because these comments linger because they are often repeated to other staff members. What executives say and how they say it make powerful impressions on employees, so preparation is always a good advice. Consider as an example the practice of an actual hospital executive: She always has in mind a general, news-related topic or a brief work-related issue that can help her along when a chance encounter with employees and physicians occur, or even during meetings where she must make impromptu or filler comments. Although this example seems stilted, it is a good preparation tool.

2. *Consider what to say in meetings carefully.* Every sentence or phrase is crucial and is subject to misinterpretation if repeated out of context. Consider the caution that politicians exercise in campaign speeches. They fully realize the importance of each and every statement.

Maintain an appropriate demeanor. Imagine a society in which everyone felt free to express their opinions and feelings without any inhibitions or obligation to conform to a code of behavior. Most of us would agree that basic courtesy, whether sincere or not, and a sense of the appropriate are necessities for a civilized society and a civilized organization. Although I do not suggest that executives should be insincere or phony on a daily basis, they must sometimes conceal their true feelings to consistently project a positive and appropriate image in the workplace.

Professional and appropriate behavior is generally expected of executives, even during times when they may be feeling less than civilized. However, if executives find that they frequently must force themselves to behave appropriately, perhaps they should consider changing jobs because continually forcing appropriate behavior is never mentally healthy. One's external behavior should generally reflect one's genuine inner self, which is also commonly referred to as character. The following real-life dilemmas test your ability to hide your true feelings in the workplace.

- Your boss has invited you and the other executives to a party at his house. The party falls on your spouse's birthday. Will you decline the invitation and tell him why? Will you go? If you go, will your countenance reveal your true feelings?
- It is the nicest weekend of the summer and the day of the long-scheduled employee picnic. You, the vice president of operations, are expected to attend and stay the entire day to welcome staff from all three shifts. Your son has asked you to join him and his scouting troop for an overnight camping trip. You know that you cannot do both and that your son will be very disappointed if you miss the trip. Will you attend the picnic and act very pleased to be there, or will you cancel and join your son? If you attend, but cut your attendance short, will you explain why to anyone?
- You have always told employees that they should feel free to come see you whenever they have an issue or a concern, as long as they have tried first to resolve it with their immediate supervisor. One employee has been calling your administrative assistant for months to schedule an appointment with you. She has visited with you seven times in the past five months and has never raised a legitimate complaint or issue. She is a very difficult person

11

from whom to disengage, and each meeting with her takes at least an hour. However, because of her informal influence within the organization, you would prefer not to shut her off. Will you continue to see her and listen half-heartedly, or will you try to persuade her not to continue calling?

The dilemmas in some of these scenarios may have obvious answers and others may not. Certainly not all readers would handle them the same way. However, all of the scenarios demonstrate the importance of maintaining an appropriate demeanor, even when conflicts get in the way.

Confront issues directly. Effective executives are problem solvers by nature. However, some executives fall into a pattern of simply moving problems around within the organization. They send some issues to a committee, place others on the proverbial "to-do" list but never get to them, and still leave others for the next administration to solve. Many issues are also put on hold until a strategic plan is finished or are given to consultants to handle.

Such approaches are not always wrong. Using committees or consultants and buying time for some issues are often viable and appropriate strategies. However, difficulties arise when such strategies become ploys to avoid necessary decision making.

Avoidance of problems is particularly acute in interpersonal relationships. Executives may try to avoid certain personal confrontations and will often go to great lengths to postpone meetings or encounters to avoid dealing with interpersonal issues because many times these clashes can be averted if they are avoided long enough. Although sometimes procrastination is the proper approach, it is totally counterproductive at other times. As a general guideline, procrastination on interpersonal confrontations is appropriate only when a limited cooling-off period is needed or when time for fact-finding would help solve the conflict.

The protocol here requires: (1) the willingness and ability to face issues that are difficult, touchy, or sensitive; (2) the ability to identify matters of conflict or potential conflict; and (3) the ability to navigate through delicate, and sometimes dangerous, waters. This requires skill, determination, and courage, which will be discussed later in the book. To exercise these skills effectively, executives should develop a good sense of timing. They should carefully consider when issues should be brought up and when they should be postponed. Unfortunately, no book provides guidelines in this area; sensitivity, experience, and observation are the best teachers. Problem solving skills also require:

- *listening.* Effective executives are also active listeners. They know and practice good listening skills, have the ability to listen with understanding and empathy, and are willing to take the extra time necessary to be an active listener. Communications experts tell us that people often spend most of their time in meetings preparing what they are going to say next so they hear and understand very little of what others say.
- *tenacity.* Executives should be action-oriented and tenacious in getting problems identified and solved. They should constantly show high energy levels and get others to do the same.
- *courage.* Courage in the business world can be derived from several sources, but the most important source is doing one's homework so that one is knowledgeable about the situation at hand. Executives should spend time learning details. Unfortunately, too many believe that they need only concern themselves with the broad picture and can allow their subordinates to handle the details.

Practice common courtesy. Comparing the behavior executives display when they are around board members and key physicians

---

Six Principles of Business Etiquette

1. Be on time
2. Be discreet
3. Be courteous, pleasant, and positive
4. Be concerned with others, not just yourself
5. Dress appropriately
6. Use proper written and spoken language

Source: Yager, Jan. 1991. *Business Protocol: How to Survive and Succeed in Business.* New York: John Wiley & Sons.

---

with behavior they display around "less important" employees is telling of how much these executives value certain groups of people. The following are common courtesy protocols that should apply to everyone equally, from the person who signs your checks to the person who takes out your office trash.

- *Be on time.*
- *Speak politely.*
- *Do not interrupt.*
- *Pay attention during presentations.*

Learn the power of symbols and how to use them accordingly. Practically anything—words, body language, dress, an expensive fountain pen, the house or neighborhood in which one lives, the car one drives—is a representation of condition or status. Although symbols are subject to everyone's interpretation, they are powerful, meaningful methods of communication. Consider the following symbols and what each means.

- A $250,000 salary and a 40 percent bonus;
- A 35 x 40 foot office with an oversize executive mahogany desk;

- Short-sleeve shirts and polyester double-knit sports jackets;
- A master's degree from the health administration program at a major university;
- An MBA degree from a little-known university;
- An expensive black sports car;
- An executive boardroom with fine wood paneling and large, swivel, leather chairs around a gleaming mahogany table; and
- A boardroom that is off the hospital cafeteria and doubles as a room for Lamaze classes (the pictures and information for the classes stay permanently on the walls).

These and many other symbols evoke certain images and enable executives to describe persons, situations, or institutions that they may typify. Executives who are unaware of the power of symbols may find that they are sending many unintended messages. Further, executives must recognize that they work in a world in which symbols often send more signals and messages than oral or written communications.

REFERENCE

Bailey, F. G. 1988. *Humbuggery and Manipulation: The Art of Leadership.* Ithaca, NY: Cornell University Press.

Chapter Two

PROFESSIONAL IMAGE

In essence, integrity is consistency between what a manager believes, how a manager acts, and a manager's aspiration for his or her organization.

Joseph L. Badaracco, Jr., and Richard R. Ellsworth in
Leadership and the Quest for Integrity (1993)

I MAGE IS AN interpretation of a persona that is perceived, whether accurately or inaccurately, as the truth. Because an executive is always under overt and covert scrutiny by her/his "audience," building and projecting a positive professional image is necessary to lessen, and ideally ward off, misinterpretation. For a healthcare executive, these audiences are employees in all levels, whether or not they work directly under the executive; supervisors and middle managers; executive peers; patients; physicians; purchasers of services, including third-party payers and managed care groups; and the community the organization serves. Professional image signals the executive's fit within the organization; its effectiveness can be measured by what is real and what seems real (perception). Professional image is based on having a strong work ethic and having interpersonal skills, as confirmed by the following abilities:

1. ability to perform all the tasks of the office;
2. ability to set and achieve organizational goals; and
3. ability to relate well with others.

Work ethic; physical appearance and personal behavior; social skills, graces, and interactions; and character establish the professional image of an executive. Each of these factors is significant, and the protocols for building and maintaining each are explored in this chapter. This discussion of image building does not advocate false insincerity or truth distortion. Instead, it advocates the cultivation of positive attributes and characteristics.

PROTOCOLS FOR DEVELOPING AND ENHANCING A STRONG WORK ETHIC

A strong work ethic is a crucial aspect in developing a good professional image. Executives should enjoy hard work and all its products, including the sense of pride that comes with accomplishments. Executives with a strong work ethic and who work at jobs they enjoy take pleasure in coming to work each day. Their work provides meaning for their lives and enhances their psychological well-being, especially when the work they do contributes to the greater good.

Use time properly. Arriving early and staying late are hallmarks of an executive's workday. However, putting in the time merely to demonstrate dedication is not as important as putting in the time to get results. Because of the multitude of issues that descend on an executive's desk, spending a great deal of time at the office is already an inevitable fact for any executive. Although effective time management is a crucial skill, the executive should be careful to cultivate the image of a hard-working, diligent, and punctual executive who has the right to expect the same diligence from her/his employees.

Prioritize. Executives should continually evaluate priorities and reassign them when needed. An objective-based work style should become second nature.

Survey employees. Because much of the success of an executive depends on her/his interaction with and management of employees, an annual survey on employee concerns must be established. These surveys would enlighten the executive on issues, such as how employees interact with each other, that are not so apparent but could be damaging to the organizational dynamics. For example, employees or medical staff members who feel that they are not getting anywhere with senior management will often go to board members to seek resolution. Executives should take note of these interrelationships and try to anticipate how they might affect decision making.

Be tenacious. Effective executives know that not all issues will be simple, not all decisions will be clear cut, and not all mistakes and pitfalls will be avoided. The ability to bounce back and keep coming at the problems is highly prized because tenacity always overcomes almost all problems.

Serve as a role model. Perhaps the best way to inspire, lead, and ultimately succeed is to set an example for others. Many executives who were deficient in some areas in the past and who have made the required personal sacrifices to succeed can be prime examples.

Walk the talk. Executives must be able to do what they request someone else to perform. Such executives are able and willing to do the necessary work to get tasks accomplished.

Do everything as well as possible. Excellence should always be an executive's goal. Executives should maintain the high level of energy needed to do jobs correctly, and they should take the extra time to study details, to prepare a little better than others, or to cover additional ground.

Maintain enthusiasm. Executives should be as enthusiastic as possible in all that they do. People who are negative or complain frequently about how impossible things are cannot set good examples and do not have the appropriate attitudes to be strong executives.

Let work become a passion. Executives should approach their work with an intensity and a desire that signal to others that they enjoy doing it.

Go above and beyond duty. Executives should do more than just what is expected and should be constantly looking for additional ways to contribute to the success of their organizations. At times, this means volunteering to serve on extra committees and work groups.

Establish a policy on integrity. Executives must set an example to all their employees by establishing specific policies and guidelines that encourage employee integrity. Policies that prevent conflicts of interest, such as accepting gifts for personal gain, must be documented, upheld, and mutually agreed upon.

PROTOCOLS FOR MAINTAINING GOOD PHYSICAL APPEARANCE AND BEHAVIOR

Physical appearance and behavior set the stage for all human interactions. What you wear or how you smell is not merely the end result of personal hygiene or vanity, and why you avoid coughing without covering your mouth is not just polite happenstance; they are the products of your commitment to yourself. Generally, this first impression dictates the direction of a meeting and its subsequent outcome. Because the career span of an executive is punctuated, and in some cases propelled, by thousands of brief encounters, he/she must master the art of maintaining good physical appearance and behavior.

Wear appropriate clothing. In many respects, appropriate executive dress is a uniform dictated by generally accepted professional standards. These standards vary, however, according to regional or cultural practices, so discretion is key. For example, dress cowboy boots may be appropriate footwear for a male executive at a medical center in Laredo, Texas, but they would look very out of place on an executive in Boston. Similarly, although navy blue suits are generally considered proper attire for male executives in Chicago hospitals, they might seem too formal in rural facilities in which sport coats complete the usual business dress ensemble.

Although the variety of proper business attire for female executives makes difficult the task of judging the appropriateness of each piece of clothing, the same basic clothing protocol applies to them as it does to males. All executives should refrain from wearing clothes that are ill fitting; sexually suggestive; sloppy— wrinkled, missing buttons, or need repair; or simply too casual. Shoes should be in good condition, clean, and should compliment the rest of the attire. Grooming should also be considered in this equation. Executives should make sure that their hair and nails are clean, neat, and well tended. Beards or mustaches, if worn, should be trimmed regularly. Elaborate or flamboyant hairstyles and jewelry or wearing too much makeup should be avoided.

Appropriate executive attire is not intended to express an executive's individuality; after all it is a uniform. Clothes that are too individualistic, stylish, or contemporary are usually inappropriate. A safe measure of whether or not an outfit is professionally appropriate is to ask others—family, friends, peers—what they would likely notice first, you or your clothes. If the answer is the latter choice, then the outfit is not for the office.

Be careful of business casual trend. The advent of business casual or "dress-down" days has made dressing for work even more challenging. Generally, erring on the side of conservatism when dressing less formally is preferred because many board members and executives, who were schooled in traditional ways, still practice the conservative approach to dressing and may not be as accepting of the new clothing trends.

Maintain good hygiene. Although I realize that mentioning, even briefly, the significance of personal hygiene in a book for health-care executives is extremely ironic, I also submit that it is necessary. According to some executive search consultants with whom I've spoken, poor hygiene hinders many well-qualified, intelligent candidates from getting top-paying positions. In fact, these search consultants have conducted interviews in which candidates had cases of bad breath (or garlic breath); body odor; or overpowering smell of cologne, aftershave, or perfume.

Mind your personal habits and behavior. Smoking, picking one's teeth, chewing gum, talking with your mouth full, and nail biting are just a few personal behaviors that some people find offensive. Again, several search consultants have confirmed that these seemingly minor habits have caused some very competent candidates their chance at getting hired, or at least tainted their image. Some of the worst case scenarios included:

- a candidate who picked his teeth in the presence of a search consultant and CEO of the hiring organization;
- a candidate who clipped her nails in front of an administrative assistant while waiting for an interview; and

- a candidate who pulled up his socks while interviewing with a nun.

Although not all of us can look as if we just stepped out of a magazine or can be polished as if we do not harbor bad habits, we can at least try to be physically clean and well behaved everyday. Doing everything possible to maintain good physical condition can also be helpful in developing and maintaining a positive image. Paying attention to physical details and personal behavior not only mirrors our most basic competencies but prevents our more memorable experience from turning into an insensitive anecdote or a punchline of a joke.

PROTOCOLS FOR PRACTICING GOOD SOCIAL SKILLS, GRACES, AND INTERACTIONS

Today's busy, high-pressure careers have relegated the practice of common courtesy and social skills to the backseat of many careerists' consciousness. As a result, stress among executives and workers is extremely high, and people in general are becoming unwittingly immune to rude behavior.

For example, a healthcare executive embroiled in a power struggle with her medical staff may at times lash out at her administrative assistant for small offenses. The assistant, in turn, would initially understand this verbal assault and would choose to overlook the incident and not say anything to the boss. As a result, the executive is unaware of the effects of her "minor" tirade and continues to take out her frustration on her assistant, or sometimes on other lower-rank staff members. Eventually, more conflict would ensue, and all would ultimately end in a damaging way.

However, not all is lost yet. Again, by inviting and practicing these common social graces and interpersonal skills, the executive can lessen stress for her/himself, get along better with staff, and gain a sharper edge.

Show courtesy. The following are some guidelines for showing courtesy.

- *Respect service employees.* The healthcare industry has a large support service staff, such as those who work in the dietary and housekeeping departments; and all executives, at some point or another, would have contact with them. Because service employees often are paid less, and are stereotyped as having less education than do professional employees, they may be looked down upon and denied the respect they deserve. However, executives must realize and respect the value and daily contribution of these workers.
- *Project a positive attitude.* Executives should not gripe without proposing a solution. Instead, learn to take problems in stride because complaining only agitates the situation and promotes inaction. Executives must limit venting because employees are often influenced by what their leaders do.
- *Avoid excessive informality.* Working with people who have similar qualities, beliefs, and interests as you do and whom you respect and admire is truly one of the greatest advantages of the modern workplace. In the same vein, however, this familiarity can also be detrimental to the workplace when it evolves into playful or fraternal involvement, which is the case when colleagues start calling each other by nicknames, playing elaborate practical jokes on each other at work, or exchanging confidential personnel problems. The most productive work settings are those that have some formality and decorum.
- *Avoid moodiness.* Attempt to maintain an even disposition and outlook because people are easier to work with when they are not intimidated by your moods.
- *Avoid profanity and sarcasm.* Use of profanity may mean that a person is becoming too emotional about an issue

and is losing control, which, of course, is not how executives should approach problems. Profanity often is used for effect or emphasis, or to spice up routine conversations. However, senior managers should find other words and ways to accomplish this. Other workers, both peers and subordinate, may be offended by the profanity, even if they do not say so. Profanity can distract from the message and intent of verbal communication. Sarcasm is also out of place in the executive suite. If executives and managers must offer criticism or reprimands, they should not resort to sarcasm, which, like profanity, distracts from the message.

- *Listen intently.* To become better and more active listeners, executives should avoid dominating conversations and participate in a dialogue, not a monologue. Executives should also learn to show concern and empathy when others express concerns or worries, but should avoid describing their own personal experiences with similar problems. They should realize that people often simply want to express themselves and not receive a lesson on how to cope with their difficulty.

- *Maintain self-control.* Society highly values the idea of remaining calm and composed during a crisis, which is what executives must strive toward because, in many cases, losing control of a situation, could mean losing control of the attention of the group being led. Recently, a number of books, such as Daniel Goleman's *Working with Emotional Intelligence,* have been written on the subject of emotional intelligence. These books demonstrate the strong correlation between self-control and executive success.

Learn to apologize. Executives make mistakes and when they do, a gracious apology to the offended party is in order. They should strive to correct the situation and be humbled by the experience.

Use executive manners outside the workplace. Executive manners must be practiced at all times—at the golf course, on the tennis court, at the exercise club, or when driving—because executives are representatives of their management team and their organization and are always "on public display." Improper behavior outside the executive suite can have negative ramifications inside the suite.

Use caution when speaking freely. Because they are privy to confidential and sensitive information, and because their ideas and opinions carry a lot of weight, executives can "drop their guards" only with those whom they trust implicitly to be discreet. On occasion, executives confide in others or divulge information to establish a bond of trust and to encourage others to reciprocate. However, this should be done with extreme caution.

Strengthen relationships by sending notes. Thank you and congratulatory notes and cards appropriately express thoughtfulness. Any time someone has done something that helps the organization or has achieved something of merit, a note is in order. Sending such notes is an excellent way to stay in touch with others and to strengthen relationships.

Express warmth, caring, and concern. Sincere concern for others' interests and welfare prevents executives from developing an ego-centered, overly aggressive professional personality. Executives who do not show concern for others may find that others will reciprocate by showing no concern for their interests and welfare as well. Executives can demonstrate warmth, caring, and concern for others in many ways, including those discussed below.

- *Smile.*
- *Maintain eye contact.*

- *Have a sense of humor.*
- *Be liberal with praise.* A number of employee surveys have shown that one of the leading concerns among employees is the lack of day-to-day recognition from executives. Formal organization-wide recognition systems, such as award luncheons, are often ineffective at addressing this concern because what employees really want is ongoing acknowledgment. Executives can accomplish this by recognizing praiseworthy actions verbally or in writing. Peers will also appreciate sincere praise because in the highly competitive world of management praise from peers is almost nonexistent. Often, peers can be praised for nonspecific accomplishments, such as stating how much one enjoys working with someone. Peer praise can often serve to strengthen personal relationships and enhance team effectiveness.
- *Avoid cute criticism.* Criticism should always be constructive and targeted to specific behavior. When people are familiar and comfortable with one another, they tend to make cutting remarks that are supposedly offered in jest, such as comments about weight gain or loss or manner of dressing. However, such comments are facetious and may be taken negatively by the recipient who may not let on that she/he feels offended.
- *Remember names.* Here are four quick suggestions:

1. Hold on to names long enough until you can write them down later for future reference.
2. Repeat the person's name slowly when meeting them.
3. Associate the person's name with a familiar object.
4. Reintroduce yourself to avoid the embarrassment of not knowing someone's name when you see him/her in the future, and apologize if necessary.

PROTOCOLS FOR MANAGING THE ENTOURAGE

Executives must manage subordinate managers and support staff because they reflect the strengths and weaknesses of the executives as well. The following are management protocols for the executive "entourage"—employees who work directly under executive supervision.

Administrative Assistants. The administrative assistant must:

- project a professional image that reflects the professionalism of the executive's office;
- have excellent administrative skills;
- have excellent manners—should be able to handle verbal and written interactions with courtesy and tact;
- have excellent administrative skills—should produce documents that are free of typos and follow grammatical rule and proper formats. (The executive must provide them with references to consult, such as a grammar book and a dictionary.);
- maintain a neat and orderly work area—should keep their desk, bulletin boards, and surrounding areas clean and free from clutter. (Personal mementos should be discreet and kept to a minimum.); and
- know and practice and behavioral protocols.

The following protocols are useful in managing administrative assistants. Executives must:

- have frequent meetings with them to plan strategy and set priorities;
- include them in decision making;
- inform them about the philosophies and reasoning behind as many decisions as possible because information

would lessen miscommunication and confused expectations; and

- routinely conduct routine priority-setting sessions with them.

Subordinate Managers. The following principles are especially useful in working with subordinate managers. Executives must:

- explain her/his management philosophy because it will help subordinate managers better understand and support executive decisions, anticipate the executive's response to issues, and tailor their requests and actions to fit well with that philosophy; and
- share information because the more subordinate managers feel "in the know" about issues, the more they will get involved and connected to the team and the more support they will give their boss. Executives may find it useful to hold weekly meetings at which every team member relates the key items on her/his weekly calendar. Information sharing enhances teamwork because it lets the team know what each member's key issues are for the week, lets the team clarify difficult or sensitive issues on the spot, and provides motivation to start the week.

THE CORRELATION BETWEEN PROTOCOLS AND CHARACTER

In ancient times, character referred to a distinguishing mark or symbol scratched permanently on a surface. Today, character still refers to a distinguishing mark, but this time the mark is on the person. In this book, character will refer to what commands us to follow or not follow the external demands of protocols. In an ideal world, all executives would have strong characters and, thus, would behave appropriately because doing so is the natural expression of their inner selves. In the real world, however, many executives are flawed and must learn to enhance their inherent character to be able to follow proper conduct. The following are protocols for strengthening character.

Be truthful. The wrong words, especially untruths, can permanently damage executives' character and their ability to lead and influence others. Distortion, insinuation, and exaggeration are all forms of dishonesty that, unfortunately, are common practice in healthcare organizations because they ease the burden of decision making by only representing details that people would prefer to hear. These dishonest tactics are so often used that I suspect some executives are not even aware that they are bending the facts.

Honesty in many instances calls for personal judgment. Sometimes, a "white lie" is called for to prevent hurting someone's feelings. Many executives avoid answering questions directly, especially when they do not know the answers or when they want to keep information away from others.

Remember that credibility is an all-or-none proposition. Credibility is how executives convince others—superiors, peers, and subordinates—to believe in what they say and do. Executives must not allow unacceptable behavior to reduce their credibility to less than 100 percent.

Promise only what can be done. Executives should be cautious about promising, or even suggesting, anything. If they say they will do something, then they must be do it. They should avoid situations where representations are made, but not precisely fulfilled. These include informing subordinates that certain policies will be changed and telling superiors that a certain report will be delivered at a certain time.

Say no when necessary. We all tend to want to please others and tell them what they want to hear. This avoidance only raises expectation levels falsely and often causes others to misperceive that a promise or guarantee was made.

Follow up on everything. Executives should be certain to follow up with people. This should be approached with the same intensity as preparing for a board meeting or a job interview.

Maintain confidences. Confidentiality is especially important when employees provide information or raise concerns about supervisors, but wish to remain anonymous. Senior managers must keep the confidentiality of employees as a sacred trust.

Personalize decisions. Executives sometimes make global decisions for their organizations without considering their impact on the employees, which occurs with layoffs or terminations. Executives should consider the effect of their decisions first by imagining themselves as recipients, instead of givers. The human costs involved in decisions and actions are often the only ones that ultimately make or break plans and programs.

Avoid temptation. Executives should strive to eliminate or minimize potentially risky or compromising situations. For example, many executives insist on signing off on even the most minor travel expenses incurred by their staff to lessen the possibility of inappropriate expense reimbursements. Consider the following real-life temptation for one executive.

A vice president in a small hospital made a $45,000 error in personnel costs when computing a budget. He realized that there was a good chance that the error would be overlooked, so he could get away with not informing the CFO and the CEO because the budget had already been approved by the board. He knew that sometime during the year the error might surface, but he figured that with overtime and other variable expenses, the amount of the error would not seem that great. Nonetheless, the vice president decided to reveal the error to the CFO and the CEO, taking full personal responsibility for it. To his surprise, both reacted quite positively, and the CFO came up with a solution that minimized the potential impact of the error.

Chapter Three

PROFESSIONAL REPUTATION

As the competition becomes fiercer, getting or keeping a job, or being promoted, will hinge not only on how qualified you are ... but how appropriately you behave, and how much you look and act the part for that particular position.

Jan Yager in *Business Protocol: How to Survive and Succeed in Business* (1991)

ALL EXECUTIVES MUST develop and enhance a professional reputation, inside and outside the office, that both reflects their personal values and transcends the immediate needs and duties of their careers. Involvement in internal and external activities, such as membership in professional organizations and/or participation in service clubs, provides positive exposure and networking opportunities; emphasizes the executive's commitment to her/his personal and professional growth; and strengthens credibility.

Maintaining a balance between internal and external pursuits, however, is the key to maintaining the reputation. An executive who becomes too preoccupied with external activities runs the risk of neglecting internal responsibilities, which ultimately

affects the entire organization. Maintaining a professional reputation at all times is a protocol all on its own, so this chapter will
focus on how to adopt, reinforce, and apply that protocol.

BUILD A PROFESSIONAL REPUTATION OUTSIDE THE ORGANIZATION

Actively participate in local and national trade associations. Although every association provides certain benefits to its members
and are limited in their reach, their primary goals are generally
the same: to provide a forum for careerists in similar professions
and to establish a professional standard by which all members
must abide. Being aware of and involved in professional associations afford the executive the opportunity to meet various leaders
who propose new and creative approaches to existing problems.
In addition, these forums, more often than not, offer professional-
development seminars. To get the most out of the benefits of
these associations, the executive must:

- attend meetings regularly;
- become an active member on their committees;
- understand that the association may not meet every
  expectation;
- work within the association's framework to address
  specific organizational concerns;
- inform the association of issues and lobbying efforts that
  affect its membership;
- volunteer to supply facts and specific examples
  to aid efforts with legislators and other policymakers;
- serve as a reference for the association; and
- volunteer to chair and coordinate educational efforts.

Teach. Students who are interested in the same profession you are
in welcome and are grateful to instructors who have theoretical

understanding of and practical experience in real-world organizational systems. Another way of teaching is sponsoring residents or administrative fellows of healthcare administration programs. These sponsorships are great learning experiences for both you and the residents and fellows.

Support continuing research in the field. Allow health administration graduate programs to use your organization's facilities when they are conducting research workshops, and participate in discussions with faculty members and researchers.

Share successes. A success story must never end where it started; it must be retold so that it can multiply. Some executives write articles, sometimes books, about their successful programs or service lines, while other executives share their successes by teaching them at lectures or seminars.

Provide legislative input. Be aware of proposed legislation and analyze how they will affect your organization. Write Congress or your local legislative body about the impact of the legislation on your organization then invite them to familiarize them with your organization, your constituents, and their needs. However, executives must not use the occasion to complain about the conflicts that certain laws and regulations are creating for the organization. Instead, they should propose alternative legislation or action.

Participate in community and service clubs. Because healthcare executives simply do not gain their professional reputation strictly within the healthcare industry, they must also get involved in community organizations, such as the Chamber of Commerce or Rotary or Lions Club. They should attend meetings regularly and volunteer to help in activities whenever possible.

BUILD A PROFESSIONAL REPUTATION WITHIN THE ORGANIZATION

Provide goal-oriented leadership. Strong, goal-oriented executives expend enormous energy in identifying visions and mission and in ensuring that they are clearly defined and understood by all employees. They look for ways to measure progress so they stay focused on future trends and issues. Because they believe in continuous improvement, these executives set new and more difficult goals each time one is completed.

Executives must not confuse busyness with accomplishments and results. They must recognize that people can be quite busy on a day-to-day basis and yet accomplish relatively little. They must work hard to ensure that their daily activities are moving their organizations and themselves forward.

For these executives, goals must meet the following criteria:

- goals must be time-measurable;
- goals must be quantifiable; and
- goals must be relevant to the strategic direction of the organization.

Catch the "can-do" spirit. Can-do attitude is simply the mindset that no problem is insurmountable and no crisis is unsolvable. Executives who adopt this attitude cut through bureaucracy, maintain high personal standards of quality, and inspire a winning attitude in themselves and others in the organization.

A correlation does exist between getting extra projects and responsibilities and possessing a positive attitude. Employees who receive interesting and skill-enhancing work are are typically the ones with can-do attitudes. The organization's pessimists are seldom placed in authority roles and rarely participate in helping the organization make major strides forward. The premise in manufacturing that output is a function of input that can also be applied to individuals.

Take credit when credit is due. Executives should take appropriate credit for the good work that they do. If others do not know about a person's accomplishments, they cannot assign her/him appropriate and additional skill-enhancing duties.

Participate actively in all areas of the organization. Executives should regularly attend and participate in various meetings, including committee and medical staff meetings.

Executives should also be active within various employee areas because maintaining high visibility, being available to help, and showing interest in others' concerns communicate professionalism and strengthen relationships. Executives who get involved with employee activities always feel positive about their organization and responsibilities and always appreciate the contributions of others. They become known as problem solvers and bureaucracy busters. Serving as mentors to department heads and managers or spending time with them outside of traditional meetings would also increase personal influence.

Be punctual. The timely completion of assigned or promised work is a major factor in maintaining credibility.

Sell ideas. The ability to influence and persuade is critical in building a reputation because the majority of day-to-day work revolves around developing, presenting, and selling ideas and concepts.

The ideal approach to selling proposals and concepts is to start the proposal by stating the end result of the activity, and then proceed by presenting the details that support the achievement of the end result. This approach is effective because most people tend to be impatient and skeptical with linear presentations. With linear presentations, the audience generally makes an assumption and a decision even before the presentation ends. If they make the wrong assumption, then they become lost in the presentation. If they make the correct assumption, they may decide against the proposal before hearing all of the facts. Executives can enhance their selling skills by being thoroughly prepared with facts and alternative solutions to issues. They should also be prepared to compromise on various issues of concern.

Be an organizational cheerleader. Executives should always project a positive outlook because employees at all levels are easily influenced by the mindset they project. Projecting an upbeat attitude and encouraging teamwork are especially crucial when the organization is facing great challenges.

Developing a positive professional reputation goes beyond polishing an image or putting up a facade; it is greatly dependent on the person's satisfaction with her/his career because building a reputation takes a lot of hard work. (Note that, generally, people who relish their work are usually the same people who have the finest reputations).

Because the healthcare field will only continue to evolve, it would require more than stamina and knowledge from its executives, it would benefit from executives who can support its fast pace because they find satisfaction at doing so and gain enjoyment at knowing that their contributions make a difference within and outside their organizations.

This satisfaction has two foundations—self-esteem and contentment with career. People with high self-esteem are confident in their abilities, enthusiastic about getting up each morning and going to work, willing to take on additional tasks for the organization, and so glad that they have chosen their careers that they talk to others about them.

Chapter Four

ETHICAL DECISIONS

There is no right way to do a wrong thing.

Kenneth H. Blanchard and Norman V. Peale in
The Power of Ethical Management (1988)

A FTER A LONG time of being overlooked, ethics in business is finally being studied in leading graduate schools
across the United States and is now a frequent discussion or exposition topic in business journals and magazines. Many
business seminars today even provide some mention, albeit brief,
of ethical issues.

In the 1990s, discussions of ethics in healthcare were relegated
to medical–legal issues such as abortion, euthanasia, living wills,
the rationing of healthcare, and parenteral nutrition. The late
1990s introduced the era of corporate compliance as healthcare
organizations found necessary the development of formalized
programs to monitor compliance with laws and regulations. However, ethical considerations should be much broader than compliance issues, and healthcare executives should set an example
of ethical practices. The obligation to provide high-quality healthcare to patients is the healthcare industry's societal calling. Therefore, a strong emphasis on ethical caregiving is an appropriate
corollary to the industry's societal obligation and responsibility.

Healthcare organizations tend to follow one another's lead. When one organization develops and establishes a service, program, or product line, such as a women's health clinic, others soon add it. If one organization acquires a certain piece of equipment or begins to advertise, not long afterward a nearby organization will follow suit. In human resources, when one organization adds a benefit or a special wage differential, other organizations in the area do the same. As a result of all this copying, these healthcare organizations start to seem alike to the public. To combat the confusion, some organizations make an effort to differentiate themselves. For example, an organization might differentiate itself by emphasizing its strong managerial ethics; after all, having a strong ethical orientation sends a different message to its consumers, physicians, and employees. As a result of this differentiation, the organization may become more successful than its competitors. However, the increase of market share should not be the reason for the development of an ethical environment; ethics should be practiced because doing so is right, not because doing so is profitable. Executives who want to make their organizations stand out from the rest must constantly try to set good examples by conducting themselves as if someone were watching all the time. The belief that one can get away with unethical behavior because no one is watching, or because a minor lapse in judgment really will not hurt anyone, can damage careers.

This chapter sets forth protocols intended to help executives make appropriate ethical choices and decisions.

THE BASIC PROTOCOL OF ETHICS

Executives must approach ethical issues with a basic protocol: Follow the three angles of organizational ethics below.

1. *Follow an organizational code of ethics.* The organizational code of ethics is either established by a committee of the board of

trustees or authored by the CEO, and must be clearly written, or published so that the entire organization is aware of it. The mission statement of an organization may also include a policy statement that mandates and encourages ethical behavior. At a minimum, the organization should have a published policy on the acceptance of gifts and gratuities, or conflict of interest. Too often, however, these policies are ignored because they do not set forth specific behavioral expectations.

Corporately prescribed ethical behavior does not stop with individual behavior; it should include protocols for how an organization should respond in the event that the organization-becomes embroiled in a public or private crisis. An example of such a protocol was employed by McNeil, the makers of Tylenol, to respond to the fatal tampering of its Tylenol capsules. McNeil immediately recalled all similar products from the shelves, offered money-back guarantees, set up a toll-free number to accommodate questions and assuage fears, and quickly pioneered new packaging techniques. Although this response protocol was a great expense, it was viewed as a highly ethical response and it possibly saved Tylenol from a bigger public-relations dilemma.

2. *Adhere to a professional code of ethics.* Every profession has a code of ethics, whether published or tacit. These codes, however, are only as good as the sanctions set up to enforce them and the willingness of the professionals to sincerely subscribe to them and police themselves. Healthcare executives should be familiar with the code of ethics of the professional association solely dedicated to advancing the executive's causes—the American College of Healthcare Executives (ACHE). ACHE's code addresses many of the global ethical dilemmas faced by executives and suggests guidelines for appropriate behavior. Conflict of interest is also discussed in this code, which advises executives to conduct themselves in the best interests of the organizations they serve, to accept no gifts offered to sway decisions, and to advise authorities of internal and external conflict of interest situations.

3. *Maintain ethical decision-making standards.* Certain ethical situations demand consistent responses over time. Ethical executives are the most effective and contribute the most. Because their personal interests are consistent with the needs of their organization, their behavior will not result in a fatal flaw that harms their leadership effectiveness. Being ethical does not mean that someone is always right. It does not mean that in every situation the decision one makes or the action one takes is inviolate. What being ethical means in this context is that:

- executives should give serious consideration to the ethical implications of their decisions;
- executives should have a personal code of ethics that they will not violate in decision making; and
- decisions should be made relative to the good they provide to groups of people as a whole and not only for the benefit of the individual.

The protocols for ethical behavior discussed below attempt to establish absolutes. In a world dealing with ethical imperatives, "grading on the curve" does not exist. Ethical behavior falls into an either-or category—it either is or is not ethical. Although in managerial life answers are not always easy and clear-cut, setting forth principles that allow no leeway or license is necessary.

GENERAL OFFICE PROTOCOLS

Do not use office stationery and postage. Executives should not use office stationery and postage for personal correspondence, especially when they are involved in a job search. Cover letters, resumes, or any personal correspondence should not be printed on company letterhead or sent using the company's postage meter. Organizational stationery and postage may be used, however, for recruiting purposes.

Do not use petty cash. Use of the petty cash fund should be clearly documented and monitored, so abuse does not take place. Executives and her/his staff must avoid use of these funds for personal reasons. An approval system is best when providing anyone access to the fund.

Do not use copy machines. A recording or payment system should be set up to allow executives to pay for their own personal copying, unless, of course, personal use is specifically spelled out as an executive benefit.

Do not use work telephones for personal long-distance calls. Executives should keep track of their personal long-distance telephone calls and reimburse the organization for them.

Do not use the support staff to perform personal errands. Unless executives own the company, their administrative assistants work for the company and not for them or their families. For example, a member of the maintenance staff should not be asked to perform maintenance tasks at an executive's home during work hours. An example of unethical and inappropriate use of staff occurred at a Midwestern hospital. Several trees were cut down on the hospital's property. The groundskeepers were instructed to cut the wood into fireplace-sized logs and deliver half to the CEO's home and half to the COO's home.

GENERAL BEHAVIOR PROTOCOLS

Keep information confidential. Comments made in confidence must be kept confidential. People who give the information have the right to expect confidentiality. However, sometimes, observing strict confidentiality prevents an executive from taking action to solve a problem. One approach to this dilemma is to remind the individual who requests confidentiality that if the statements

43

must be kept in strict confidence, nothing can really be done about solving the problem or ameliorating the situation. Executives should be certain they do not leave the impression that they can or will do something in these cases. This understanding will temper the expectations of the person sharing the information as well as protect the confidentiality of that informant.

Do not accept anything of value. This protocol is probably the one most frequently violated by all executives; most people make exceptions to this rule. The exceptions usually involve allowing consultants or others to buy lunches or dinners or accepting small gifts from vendors or others. The potential problem with this is not knowing where to draw the line.

Do not take credit for other's work. When subordinates do work that is well received in the organization, executives must give them the appropriate credit and should let them know when others express praise for the work.

Follow organizational rules. Executives should abide by the rules that govern every single employee in the organization and not abuse their power by making exemptions. They should not expect to get special treatment such as receiving their paychecks early. Consider the good example illustrated by this actual case: A hospital had a temporary parking shortage and asked all employees to park on surface lots several blocks from the hospital. One of the hospital executives had a reserved space in the parking garage adjacent to the hospital, but during the shortage, he parked in the less-convenient, off-site lot along with the rest of the employees.

In many organizations, unethical practices result from a sense of executive privilege. Consider the following example: All middle managers in one organization were supposed to work as if they were paid on an hourly basis, although their hours were not monitored as such. One middle manager took time off every two weeks to get a haircut, which he justified to himself by explaining, "It grows on hospital time! I'll get it cut on hospital time." Although this example is extreme—because few hospitals have their managers working on an hourly basis—the meaning is pertinent.

Act as if someone is always watching. Executives should consider themselves to be under scrutiny always and be able to justify their actions in ethical terms. An executive's reputation and credibility are always subject to challenge so she/he should never let her/his guard down. Simply put, when in doubt, do not do it.

The ultimate cause of unethical behavior is selfishness. Giving to and sharing with others will ward off a lot of behavior that borders on the unethical. Executives should attempt to make a contribution to society when making decisions and must take actions that benefit the greatest number of people (although, certainly, exceptions to this rule exist). Services provided in a healthcare setting should be viewed by society as being on a higher order than that of other businesses and industries.

Chapter Five

INTERPERSONAL RELATIONSHIPS

The soul of effective interpersonal relations is empathy. Empathetic managers and employees express to others a sense of understanding and compassion for their emotions and feelings.

Stephen Strasser in *Working It Out: Sanity and Success in the Workplace* (1988)

I NTERPERSONAL SKILLS ARE seldom taught, rarely discussed, and infrequently included in management development programs or addressed in business journals or periodicals. The main reason for this lack is that interpersonal skills are difficult to teach because they are not easily quantifiable, and executives tend to avoid focusing on developing skills that are not concrete and objective. In most organizations, as long as the measurable portions were going well, success is thought to be evident and all other factors are ignored. Even union organizational efforts are seldom viewed as problems that resulted from interpersonal skills issues.

Most executives would agree that the ability to get along with people is one of the factors in a successful leadership. However, the same executives may not put this belief into action. Consider the following problems that result from lack of interaction between executives and employees.

- Many employees are intimidated by the executives in their organizations and seldom see them as real people. Employees who express their honest opinions and feelings about their organization's executives speak with disgust and aversion.
- Many surveys today about organizational attitudes show that executives, in all industries, have less credibility than ever before. Most executives are so distant from the rank and file that they have little sense of what is really occurring in their own organization.
- Many executives are uncomfortable with the rank and file.

Good interpersonal skills are also important in dealing with peers and supervisors. For executives, the ability to get along must be as important as getting results. Although proven methods for developing stronger interpersonal skills do not exist, the protocols discussed below may help.

GENERAL PROTOCOLS FOR IMPROVING INTERPERSONAL SKILLS

Acquiring and strengthening interpersonal skills are dependent on being aware and honoring all people, not just those who are like us or those who serve us. Recognize others by:

- being selfless;
- putting others ahead of you often, if not always;
- being sympathetic to others' situations;
- being willing to give and share; and
- trying to make others feel comfortable.

Avoid favoritism. Favoritism breeds dissension, resentment, and unhealthy competition. Executives need every employee's help so they cannot be perceived as favoring one person over another. If executives fall into this foible, the organizational grapevine will immediately identify employees who are "in" and "out". This will distract the organization from making positive strides toward its goals.

Be direct. Executives must strive to be known for their forthrightness or candidness in all their organizational dealings. This unfailing straightforwardness helps develop and maintain good interpersonal relationships.

Practice face-to-face interactions. When possible, executives should deal with people face to face because these types of encounters help nullify negative feelings. With rare exceptions, these interactions minimize negative feelings and transform them into more positive outcomes and energies. Body language and facial expressions more often communicate truer expressions and enhance understanding. Busy executives should resist the temptation to telephone instead of visit. They should take the time to walk to the offices and work locations to meet their constituent.

Be consistent. Executives should apply one rule and should say and mean the same message to everyone, regardless of her/his rank or power, all the time. Executives must remember what they have done or said so they can remain consistent in the face of questioning or doubt.

Deliver criticisms privately and constructively. Although this protocol is very simple and basic, it is often violated, especially in staff meetings. Some executives think that if their criticism is not a formal disciplinary statement or if it were intended as a motivational barb, then it can be done in front of peers. Some executives may also believe that negative comments made in open meetings are a managerial rite of passage. The executives may think that if their managers cannot understand and take the comments, then they should not be in managerial positions. Executives must remember how these casual, public barbs affected them as they were climbing the organizational ladder; an executive who would honestly say that they appreciated and benefited from these criticisms is rare.

People should be told a reason that they are being criticized. Executives should outline specific fault in behavior or speech rather than generally attack personal characteristics. When criticizing, executives should offer assistance in correcting the problem to ensure that the criticism is not merely arbitrary but constructive. Executives should not follow up their criticism of poor job performances by stepping in and doing the work themselves. Consider the following illustration of how criticisms can alienate others.

- One newly hired CEO of a Midwestern organization criticized some of his team members in front of the entire team. As a result, two of the managers who were stronger members, whom the CEO criticized, left the team. Although the CEO intended the end result, he also so alienated the other members, whom he wanted to stay, that they, too, eventually left.
- Another CEO brought four of her vice presidents into her office following their presentations at a board meeting and screamed at them for what she considered to be poor presentations. Three of these executives quit within a year.

SPECIFIC PROTOCOLS FOR IMPROVING INTERACTION WITH SUBORDINATE MANAGERS

An executive's immediate subordinates are usually managers themselves and are important contributors to the executive's success. These subordinate managers serve as "extensions" or surrogates and usually display similar drive and goal orientation as their executives. Being on the executive's team becomes increasingly important to the subordinate manager as she/he climbs the organizational ladder because the higher the rank of her/his executive, the more power and influence she/he has.

Unfortunately, however, executives do not always show their subordinate managers the same respect and consideration that they show their lower-level subordinates. Possible reasons for this disparity may include the old adage "familiarity breeds contempt," the executive's feeling of power, or the executive's possible disapproval of either the subordinate manager's ascent into the position that the executive used to occupy or the subordinate manager's poor handling of the office. The following true stories illustrate why cultivating a strong interpersonal relationship between executives and their subordinate managers is crucial.

- The CEO of a Southern organization would frequently lose his temper in such an explosive fashion that his vice presidents spent vast amounts of time covering for one another's mistakes and hiding negative news to avoid the CEO's outbursts. When the subordinate managers were invited to participate in the recruitment interview of executive candidates, they described in detail for the candidates the explosive nature of the CEO. As a result, several good candidates who might otherwise have joined the organization rejected offers of employment.
- The CFO of a Midwestern teaching hospital had a tendency to stare intently at people who were talking to him. His staring made most people very uncomfortable, especially because he did not offer an occasional recognition of points, via physical or verbal gesture, to indicate that he was listening or understanding. After a person finished talking, the CFO let several seconds of silence elapse

before responding. Some of his subordinates often wondered whether or not he was listening; others simply thought that his staring and silence were forms of psychological intimidation.

- A vice president of nursing at an Eastern hospital would frequently call nurse managers into her office and berate them for small issues she noticed during rounds, such as leaving carts or equipment in the halls of the unit. At all other times, the vice president was a good listener and a fair manager.
- The CEO at a large health system would frequently ask her subordinates about their families and personal lives. However, after they responded, she would quickly change the subject back to work-oriented issues. Her subordinates found her interest with their personal lives superficial and that she used these fleeting exchanges as segues to other topics.

Subordinates' desire and ability to perform is strongly influenced by how their executives relate to them. The protocols below will help the executive build a strong interpersonal relationship with her/his subordinate managers.

Nurture their personal and professional interests. Helping subordinates learn and subsequently advance in their pursuit of personal or professional goals build a strong network of support and encourages loyalty and diligence from them. Many successful executives have nurtured the careers of their subordinates who have gone on to become executives themselves.

Do not humiliate them. Mocking, either jokingly or seriously, and any types of humiliation, either privately or publicly, is extremely destructive to interpersonal relationships. Although maintaining a comfortable professional distance from employees is important, showing them that they are valued as individuals is likewise essential.

Get to know them. Executives who know about her/his subordinates' personal lives—their families, their problems, and their interests—develop a deeper understanding and concern. This relationship is stronger and encourages loyalty. Of course, personal information must be volunteered by the subordinate and only shared if doing so is not uncomfortable.

Apologize gracefully. Everyone occasionally makes errors or mistakes. When necessary, executives should make amends to subordinates.

Be tactful and diplomatic. Always consider others' sensitivities and preferences. Anything less is boorish.

Support them. Subordinates must be provided not only with proper information with which to do their jobs, but also with ample support. Withholding information is a way to assert power, and denying support discourages open exchange of ideas and thwarts interpersonal growth. If executives disagree or cannot support the subordinate, she/he must offer an explanation or alternative.

Ask for feedback. Executives can get meaningful feedback on their leadership styles, strengths, and weaknesses by employing 360-degree evaluation systems. A good time to obtain such feedback is just before a subordinate manager leaves an organization. A number of leading executives believe that people are often more willing to appraise or criticize their executives when they are about to leave their positions.

Chapter Six

THE WORK FORCE

In the future, the source of human achievement will not be
extraordinary individuals, but extraordinary combinations of
people—in business, science, politics, and the arts.

Robert Hargrove in *Mastering the*
Art of Creative Collaboration (1998)

MANY MANAGEMENT LITERATURE not only honor
the important contribution of a dedicated, competent work force, but also recognize that organizational
success is not possible without the work force's support of the
organizational mission. Most healthcare executives agree with
this summation. With the growing shortages of registered nurses,
allied health technologists, and other key staffers, recruiting, re-
taining, and motivating a supportive rank and file are necessary.

Because of differences in lifestyle, education, and cultural and
socioeconomic background, many executives think that they do
not have a lot in common with many of their employees; therefore, many executives are often uncomfortable with approach-
ing their staff, and hence either act awkward or too polished in
their presence. Whether or not we like the situation, class distinction exists in the United States, which is exemplified in the
power structure of any organization. This class distinction seeps

into our subconscious and affects the way we think, play, and work. For example, when you imagine the recreational habits of your organization's male CEO, what images pop into your mind? Many people would imagine that the CEO plays golf on an expensive, private country club, which could and could not be true. What would you imagine to be the recreational habits of a female administrative assistant? Shopping maybe? Would you imagine bowling or watching football for a male security guard? Would you imagine that the CEO has more expensive clothing or accessories in her/his closet than a registered nurse would? Further, what do you imagine executives talk about with their families at the dinner table? Do you think their conversations are loftier than the banter between a receptionist and her/his children? Unfortunately, these stereotypical images prevent many of us—executives and line workers alike—from interacting and beget the discomfort and intimidation we feel when faced with workers or bosses with whom we do not normally socialize. Instead of learning how to overcome these feelings, however, many of us avoid the interaction altogether, which has become a typical response to the issue.

Some executives are distant in and out of the office. They only see their employees in the organization when they need something done and only come in contact with the employees' families at the annual picnic. In turn, some employees are equally distant and harbor ill will for their executives whom they label to be insincere or manipulative (again, perception is more important than reality). A more complicated interaction conflict comes to play when a rank-and-file employee climbs up the organizational ladder. When this promotion happens, interaction between the new executive and her/his former coworkers become strained and harder to maintain because the new executive starts taking on the work, the power, and mindset of the executive staff. Subsequently, the former colleagues of the new executive, who once was "one of the girls/boys," start to perceive a change in attitude. To be fair, however, actual cases prove that some executives make a valiant attempt at interacting with their employees, but their efforts are stunted when the employees themselves push them away. Consider the following examples.

- Several vice presidents at a Midwestern hospital tried to work themselves into the employee golf league. The executives were registered on the substitute list, but were never called to play. When one of the vice presidents asked an employee in the league why they were never called to substitute, the employee replied: "Most of the guys are just not comfortable with having VPs play with us."
- The vice president of human resources of a hospital in the East joined the staff bowling league. He found that many of the employees seemed uncomfortable around him. His suspicion was confirmed when several of the employees later told him that he reminded them too much of work and that they would prefer that he not bowl in their league.

Of course, in many organizations the executives and the rank and file interact well professionally and socially. This successful interaction happens because both parties are open and willing to accommodate each other. The problem with interaction appears when it is forced. Executives sometimes make a mistaken generalization: The rank and file wants to socialize with them. Enforced fraternizing is usually a misguided strategy. The following protocols can help executives improve their working relationship with the rank and file.

Abandon the "open-door" policy. For years, executives were taught that they need to make themselves available to employees via an open-door system—a certain time when employees can meet with them in their offices. This policy dictates that employees must not go through levels of management to obtain a management-level response or assistance; instead, employees must have ready access to executives. The open-door policy has become a major component in the success of many employee-relations practices.

However, the policy itself is symbolic of managerial power in that it requires the employee to come to the manager, in contrast to the manager going to the employee. Although some employees may feel free to avail themselves of this opportunity, many more do not. Executives must not forget that most employees do not feel comfortable in the executive suite or coming to it.

A logical solution to a possible "ivory tower" syndrome is to "manage by walking around" (MBWA). Although the objective of MBWA is to visit employees and sites, some executives misunderstand the concept and perform it by doing a rather cursory and superficial walk through. Employees have come to expect and barely tolerate these tours. The following protocols enhance this concept and offer alternatives to the open-door policy.

- *Leave the office regularly and frequently.* Executives should get out into the organization and spend as much time as possible with the employees on their own turf. They should consider the possibility of working with certain departments for four-, six-, or even eight-hour periods and rotate through several departments over a period of months. One CEO keeps in his office a number of uniforms from different departments and frequently dons them to work in different departments.
- *Have lunch or share breaks frequently with the rank and file.* Executives should go to the employee cafeteria to sit with various groups of employees. Such encounters can offer the executive amazing amount of information and insights into the employee mindset. Many executives pride themselves on the fact that they lunch with a selected group of employees each month to enhance communications and understanding. This is an excellent practice, but should not take the place of informal opportunities to mix with

employees. Although many employees enjoy these formal opportunities, others may perceive these occasions as just another free lunch for the executive.

• *Make off-shift visits.* To truly get a sense of their work life, executives should visit the night shift at a busy time. Executives should also consider spending an entire shift with the night staff.

Take extra time to listen. During your interaction with employees, listening in depth to their concerns will pay valuable dividends. Employees often bring up issues and problems gradually over the course of the conversation and in the process carefully check the executive's reactions. If they are interrupted too early in the process, they may never get to their real concerns. Many executives try to solve specific problems, only to find out later that those were not the real problems. Keep in mind that real or perceived barrier between executives and the rank and file will always exist.

Initiate a job-shadowing program. A job-shadowing program allows an employee to spend an entire working day with an executive; in turn, the executive also spends an entire day with the employee at her/his job. Job-shadowing programs differ from the department-rotation concept in that they are more tailored to the employee's interest and involve a person-to-person interaction. These programs can also be developed in a formalized manner to enhance the understanding of a particular job or unit. Another benefit for the executive is that she/he develops sources of information through the organizational grapevine.

Do not touch other employees. A handshake is the only appropriate form of physical interaction in a business setting because it is the least subject to misinterpretation. Confining touching to handshakes is more than just an excellent rule in avoiding sexual harassment charges; it makes great business sense.

Many executives tend to touch employees when offering praise or giving instruction. For example, they may offer a pat on the back or put their arm around an employee's shoulders. Although the intent is not malicious, these contacts can be problematic. First, these contacts suggest a parent-child relationship. The work setting should reflect an adult–adult alliance, and many employees, although they may not express it, feel that they are being treated like children when patted or touched in this fashion.

Second, these actions imply that one party—the executive— has greater power, which is certainly contrary to the popular leadership philosophy of employee empowerment. Therefore, the last thing that executives should do is make employees feel inferior because such feelings could make employees doubt the executive's intent to make them partners in achieving the organizational mission. To prevent sending the wrong message, executives should try to become familiar with the cultures and attitudes represented within the organization. Not touching is better than offending an employee. Instead of touching, executives can "touch" employees with a smile, a compliment, public praise, or handwritten notes.

Use caution when making unplanned comments. Executives should choose their words carefully when they are with groups of employees and avoid poorly thought-out comments that might be misinterpreted. They should be equally cautious when giving criticisms and to target the undesirable behavior, not the person, in private. Executives tend to give directions or orders, especially during their walks through the organization. The rank and file often perceives such guidance as criticism, and may make comments such as " What does she know? How long has it been since she has done any real work?"

Be positive and optimistic. Management consultant Marilyn Moats Kennedy teaches that although executives do not always need to "feel" the role, they must always "act" the role of being optimistic. Executives should examine their approaches to employees and the atmosphere they create. This is particularly true when they are doing such ordinary and routine things as coming in from the parking lot or picking up their lunch from the cafeteria. Many employees value these opportunities to see the executives and derive a certain amount of inspiration and encouragement from them. These are excellent opportunities for executives to generate enthusiasm for the organization and its programs.

One common element found in almost all excellent executives is their positive energy. They always seem willing and anxious to challenge all problems and issues. These managers enjoy the opportunity to try every approach possible to deal with difficulties. Their positive attitude is contagious and spreads through the organization. The following protocols are effective in increasing positive energy.

- *Do not complain.* The rank and file typically sees executives as occupying enviable positions so they do not understand why executives complain. Badmouthing or making unwarranted negative comments about situations or people can be very counterproductive and should be avoided if they have no constructive value.
- *Adopt a can-do attitude.* Individuals who have a can-do attitude can break the bureaucracy and get things done.

Chapter Seven

EXECUTIVE TEAM MEMBERS

People on real teams must trust and depend on one another—
not totally or forever—but certainly with respect to the team's
purpose, performance goals, and approach. For most of us,
such trust and interdependence do not come easily; it must
be earned and demonstrated repeatedly if it is to change
behavior.

Jon R. Katzenbach and Douglas K. Smith in
*The Wisdom of Teams: Creating the High-
Performance Organization* (1993)

ALTHOUGH COMPETING FOR scarce resources is human nature, the practice is almost always harmful. The
growing number of healthcare administrators seeking
top positions in organizations match the increased competitiveness within the organizations among executives vying for positions that would further their careers. For top executives, the
challenge is minimizing this competitiveness to salvage personal
camaraderie and increase organizational productivity and effi-
ciency. The key to successfully reducing this selfish organizational mindset is to start from the top: Assemble a team that consists of competent executives and, by constant example and
teaching, encourage each member to set aside her/his personal
agenda for overall good of the organization. The logic here is if

the method works at the top, it would certainly trickle to all areas of the organization. This chapter prescribes protocols that are intended to improve relationships among team members to ultimately decrease the proliferation of competitive mindset.

First, however, consider two common products of competitiveness that result in team friction and poor interaction: (1) jealousy and envy and (2) tunnel vision. These shortcomings, if uncontrolled, can be destructive to an organization and its team-building efforts.

JEALOUSY AND ENVY

Jealousy is a product of unhealthy rivalry between individuals, and frequently appears when unequal standards for gaining recognition and rewards are perceived. The following are some areas in which jealousy takes root.

- Organizational reporting structure. In some organizations, vice presidents report to different top executives— COO or CEO. This differentiation can lead to jealousy because CEOs are typically higher ranked, so those who report to her/him are perceived to have a better advantage. Problems about reporting also surface when the subordinate manager's area of expertise dictate to whom she/he reports. For example, in some organizations, the CFO reports to the CEO, and the chief marketing officer reports to the COO. These problems in reporting have increased over the past decade with the growth of multi-corporate arrangements. Sometimes, simply adding the title "senior" to certain positions—for example, senior vice president—can cause jealousy.
- Organizational resources. Imbalance in distribution of available money, supply, manpower, etc., is particularly sensitive. For example, some vice presidents become jealous of the vice president of nursing because they think

that she/he receives more resources and, therefore, has a better advantage.

- Organizational budget. CFOs are often the target of this jealousy because they are not only in charge of the purse strings, they are also privy to sensitive salary information.
- Organizational hierarchy. Staff executives often believe that they are subordinate to line executives. As a result, staff executives create control mechanisms within their areas of responsibility to increase their influence.
- Organizational responsibilities. Many executives are plagued by the desire to have more power or authority over more departments or more employees. Of course, a certain amount of this acquisitive attitude is what gives executives the drive to aspire to more responsible executive positions. This attitude can be negative, however, if not placed in proper perspective.

One suggestion for minimizing the negative effects of jealousy is to create an environment in which all executives fully understand and appreciate one another's role. One way to accomplish this is to have all executives, rather than just line executives, take administrative call and make executive rounds. By doing this, staff executives will gain an increased understanding of line issues.

Another suggestion is to have a staff executive cover for a line executive who is on vacation, and vice versa. For example, the vice president of marketing should serve as the backup for the vice president of professional and clinical services, and vice versa. During vacations, the backup would literally occupy the other executive's office for a length of time, hold the regular departmental meetings, and supervise the departmental managers of the area. One CEO who employed this role-trading method reported that the two executives involved developed a much closer relationship and now work better as a team. Envy, on the other hand, stems from resenting and coveting others' resources or talents, and can be destructive to a team. Covetousness causes people to want others' possession—whether tangible or intangible—so badly that the desire eclipses all other activities. The following are the tangibles and intangibles that executives can be envious about.

- Space—office or departmental area.
- Staff—FTEs.
- Access to CEO—reporting relationship, nearby office, or time spent.
- Access to the board—attendance at meetings.
- Access to information.
- Equipment—personal: car phone, home fax machines; or departmental: computers.
- Responsibility and authority.
- Department or cost center.

All people are envious at times; however, when envy becomes extreme and all consuming it jeopardizes the team atmosphere. Furthermore, it isolates and decreases sharing of information and resources, all of which are detrimental to the team, its members, and the organization.

TUNNEL VISION

Tunnel vision is the tendency to view only a single dimension or to view one area as more important than others. Healthcare executives are no more immune to tunnel vision than are executives in other industries. In fact, one might argue that the high degree of specialization of most healthcare executives makes them especially prone to tunnel vision; many executives, especially chief nursing officers, have come up the organizational ladder via a specialist track. Other than those who have been line executives, true healthcare generalists are rare. Even in those rare cases, line executives rarely have staff experience in human resources, marketing, or finance.

Tunnel vision is problematic in situations with high-stakes payoffs and penalties. In these cases, executives with tunnel vision typically retreat to their own areas of expertise and identify problems and possible solutions from that single perspective. Consider the following examples.

- If an organization faces serious financial difficulties and must institute across-the-board budget cuts, many executives will do anything possible to protect their own areas. This protective instinct is not always done for selfish reasons but because the executive's tunnel vision prevents them from seeing the bigger organizational picture. One nursing executive in a major teaching hospital customarily kept large numbers of budgeted vacancies in the nursing labor-expense budget so that she could overhire additional nurses whenever experienced nurses applied at the medical center. During the 1980s, the hospital went through several attrition-reduction programs and eliminated a number of vacant lines. The nursing executive was able to cut several full-time employees (FTEs) without suffering any inconvenience. This tunnel-vision approach was very detrimental to team effectiveness in this situation.
- Problems arise when executives believe that the solution falls only under their jurisdiction. For example, many human resources executives believe that compensation issues fall exclusively in their domain. They will constantly take charge of the overall compensation program and often, as a result, they get little buy-in, and sometimes blame, from other executives when changes in the compensation program are made.
- Executive teams are faced with so much issues that each member must focus on her/his own particular areas to

expedite decision making; little information- and idea sharing often take place. Therefore, each team member does not consider issues that do not directly and immediately affect her/him and, hence, does not consider the ripple effect of someone's decisions.

Healthcare executive Michael H. Covert told his executive team that he expected them to act as though they were COOs when they sat at the administrative table. He asked his administrative staff to represent their own areas of responsibility, but to take on a broader perspective when the time came to make decisions as a team.

PROTOCOLS FOR WORKING WITH TEAM MEMBERS

The following protocols are designed to improve interaction and teamwork among executives and increase the overall effectiveness of the organization.

Share information. Building sources of power and developing areas of influence by withholding information and using information as a product to be traded for personal gain jeopardize teamwork. Competent executives should be confident enough to share information appropriately at all times. They should know that sharing information will assist them in the pursuit of their goals because one must share information to get information.

Encourage healthy conflict. Healthy controversy and confrontation should be encouraged, not repressed because it is a natural outgrowth of any interaction. By doing so, the concerns that cause the conflict can at least surface. Executives must stimulate healthy conflict and must resolve it in a professional and team-spirited manner. See Figure 7.1 for protocols on fighting fair.

Figure 7.1: Ten Ways to Fight Fair

1. Fight based upon facts, not emotions.
2. Present true and appropriate facts about the dispute. Each team member must be allowed to challenge the validity of those facts and present counterpoints and, in turn, must be open to appropriate challenges and must be willing to accept correction when relevant.
3. Listen to the opposition.
4. Do not gunnysack. "Gunny sacking" means raising a barrage of past arguments and no-longer-relevant issues. Another form of gunny sacking is bringing up past problems that were solved because of one's willingness to compromise. The gunny sacker is quick to remind everyone of her/his past sacrifices. In doing so, she/he is trying to gain concessions from others because they have supposedly already made their own concessions.
5. Do not turtle. A "turtler" does not do much debating during the conflict but instead remains quiet. Often, this person will wait until an agreement is reached to raise issues and complain that not all issues were considered. Also, a turtler will later on sabotage any agreement reached or distort the true arrangements of the outcome.
6. Argue the issue, not the personalities or the environment.
7. Be assertive, not aggressive. Present the points within the context of a debate, not in a combative fashion.
8. Fight soon. Air your disagreements sooner rather than later. Do not allow issues to simmer below the surface.
9. Be prepared to compromise. When the conflict is over and an agreement has been reached, repeat the terms and conditions of the agreement once again before ending the session.
10. Recognize formal and informal team roles. Executives should remember that each team member brings a different expertise and set of skills.

Establish accountability. The assignment of responsibility ensures that something gets done. Two potential conflicts over accountability surface in teamwork. The first conflict results when too many executives want responsibility for an area or function; the second one results when no executive wants responsibility for an area or function. The CEO or COO must clearly delineate organizational structure and the rationale behind assignment of accountability. Failure to do so would result in conflicts at all levels of the organization. The rank and file often solves a lot of minor accountability problems. Sometimes, however, more serious conflicts are pushed up within the organizational hierarchy and end up facing the executives. Organizational charts are developed in part to delineate the hierarchy of accountability, but they are not enough. The aggressive sponsorship of the CEO or some other governing head is required to clarify responsibilities, set forth clear lines of authority, and discuss potentially overlapping responsibilities.

Chapter Eight

GOVERNING BOARD

Board work is tough and important work; it is done by part-time volunteers who must direct and oversee large and incredibly complex organizations operating in an industry and markets undergoing profound change.

Dennis D. Pointer and James E. Orlikoff in *Board Work: Governing Health Care Organizations* (1999)

C OURTS OF LAW, government regulatory agencies, and JCAHO all look to the governing board as the ultimate authority on the operations of a healthcare organization. Governing boards have several basic responsibilities; the first of them is "preserving the institution's assets" by managing it in accordance with sound business principles. This responsibility is accomplished by (a) overseeing financial condition, (b) ensuring the appropriateness of contractual agreements, (c) obtaining adequate business and liability insurance coverage, (d) preventing and guiding through legal entanglements, and (e) supervising the collection of revenues. Most boards perform these functions through committees. For example, financial activity is reviewed by the board's finance committee. The second responsibility is ensuring the provision of adequate and competent patient care by employing skilled caregivers, especially the medical staff. The board must establish mechanisms for reviewing credentials prior to granting practice privileges to physicians, and must institute methods to review the quality of care given in the organization. The third responsibility, and perhaps the most important, is selecting the organization's CEO. Accomplishing this responsibility often causes conflict among board members. The fourth, and final, is fiduciary responsibility. Because the corporation's board has the ultimate authority on all its functions, it is ultimately liable for all its decisions.

The summary of these responsibilities is essential because it explicates the demands of the duty on the board, and it signals the areas in which potential power struggles between chief executives and board members could ensue. Immediate causes of power struggles range from institutional bureaucracy to personality conflicts to varying management views. The root cause, however, is the same: poor, or lack of, working and interpersonal relationships. The protocols submitted below aim to promote better relationships. Although these protocols are targeted at CEOs, they can be useful to other executives as well.

Participate in the screening of board members. Board membership in healthcare organizations is no longer an honorary position. It should not be offered as a reward for those who donate significant amounts of money to the organization. The position is time consuming and challenging, so the candidates who are right for the job must be willing and prepared to spend time learning and orienting themselves about the specific field and organization in which she/he wants to work. CEOs should be involved as much as possible in the screening of prospective board members because they are the ones with whom the members would be working. They should meet with each prospect to acquaint her/him with:

- the time commitments required by the job;
- the peculiarities and special challenges of the industry as a whole and the organization in particular;

- the mission of the organization; and
- the needs of the community the organization serves.

Prepare for conflicts of interest. The key to preparing for conflict-of-interest issues is to establish a written policy that identifies potential sources of conflict of interest and enumerates the subsequent actions that will be taken. Although you cannot guarantee that a board member will not use her/his position for personal gain, these policies are designed to protect the organization in case the situation occurs. Although having physician representation on the board is beneficial, it also creates a conflict-of-interest issue because the physician may always have a relationship with the organization and its medical staff, which could bias her/his decision making or advocacy. Physician board members often are very active, influential members of the medical staff; are financially valuable to the organization in that they admit a large number of patients; and are, most likely, extremely loyal to the organization. As a result of these ties, other board members tend to overlook positions taken by physician members and charge conflict of interest.

This area is fraught with potential problems. What should be established is a clearly written and frequently discussed conflict-of-interest policy that requires physician board members to remove themselves from any deliberations or actions that directly affect them as members of the medical staff.

Share information completely and immediately. Mechanisms should be in place to guarantee an adequate flow of information or communication among board members and between them and the CEO. CEOs should avoid presenting board members with surprises and, whenever necessary, must notify them in advance—by fax, telephone, e-mail, or messenger—of any potentially damaging news or adverse situations, so that board members do not find out about the news by chance or from outside sources.

One CEO of a Southern hospital visited each board member once a month to touch base and briefly cover the agenda of the upcoming board meeting. By doing this, the CEO not only communicated board issues but also developed a better personal working relationship with each member.

In working with a board, CEOs should guard against communicating primarily with just one member or a small group of members, which often occurs when CEOs work primarily with board executive committees. Board members who are not members of executive committees may feel left out of the decision-making process as a result.

Manage controversy. Often, controversial issues surface in the course of a meeting. Ideally, discussion on these controversial issues should be postponed until later to allow time for consensus building and to determine where members stand on the issues. Dealing with tough issues only after thorough preparation is the safest and best policy. Executives should work hard with the board officers to keep items that are not on the agenda out of the discussion. However, controversy cannot be put off forever. Difficult issues must be raised and addressed. Executives should protect their credibility by being as open and honest as possible with board members.

Respect board members' time and schedules. Busy CEOs should understand that board members are also busy and that the time members spend at board meetings is time taken away from their families, careers, and pockets. Therefore, all meetings should start on time and should run as efficiently as possible. Tardiness and longer-than-planned meetings should never occur. Many successful CEOs arrange with their board chairs to allocate time for each item on the agenda. Thus, each presenter and each board member knows in advance the time allotted for each topic.

CEOs should send relevant reading material, which should be complete and free or errors, to all board members far enough in advance to give them a chance to review and study. Each article should, when at all possible, have a summary attached to it so that the members can quickly grasp each issue before exploring the detail.

Whenever possible, meetings should be held at the places of business of board members because doing so shows the members the ultimate respect for and consideration of their time. Also, board members often will feel more comfortable meeting off site and will accomplish more. Off-site meetings usually minimize interruptions and will provide the CEO with an opportunity to see the members' places of business. When members visit the organization, the CEO and executives should see them promptly and offer as much hospitality as possible. The CEO should remind the staff of the importance of respecting members' time, talents, and willingness to serve.

Provide ongoing education. Regular and meaningful ongoing education of board members can be an important way to develop and maintain positive relationships because many problems stem from a simple lack of practical knowledge. Unfortunately, many boards do not take the time for regular education and board development. CEOs can start an education program by offering a detailed and meaningful orientation to new board members. Too often, we mistakenly assume that meaningful board education must involve outside speakers and formal retreats at getaway locations. However, many boards have successfully implemented ongoing education by devoting a 30-minute period at the beginning of each meeting to an in-depth coverage of a specific topic. The more educated board members are about the field, the organization, and the issues confronting the organization, the more likely they are to support the CEO and her/his policies.

Coordinate all communication. To prevent miscommunication and conflict, the CEO must be the sole channel through which information between the organization (the executives) and the board passes. Although the concept is simple, some executives who work very closely with board committees ignore it by dealing directly with the board members. As a result, these executives second guess or undermine the CEO and cause conflict and unnecessary double work with inappropriate information. One-person coordination is necessary to set priorities and avoid conflicts. Executives must present a united front on common issues. Also, the CEO should closely monitor any work the staff does with various board committees to ensure its quality and completeness.

Understand board members' community roles. A good "public relations" act is for executives to contribute their own time, and perhaps money, to issues that are important to their board members. For example, if a board member is chair of the local community fund drive, the organization should participate in the drive.

Be positive about the organization's past leadership. Executives should never cast any negative light on their predecessor(s) and their administration, especially CEOs who have been brought in to accomplish a turn around. They should remember that some, or all, of the current board members may believe that the comments on the past administration cast a negative reflection on them. Board members may also feel that the negative statements about past leadership are being made to enhance present achievements. Present leaders should let their accomplishments speak for themselves. If executives receive praise for their work that is accompanied by negative comments about the past administration, the executive should accept the compliments gratefully and ignore the criticism of past leadership.

Refrain from inappropriate humor. In meetings, all executives and the overall atmosphere should be serious. Before they consider sharing humorous anecdotes or jokes, executives should keep in mind (1) the nature of the issues with which the board deals; (2) the fundamental nature of the board's fiduciary responsibility; and (3) the diversity of implicit beliefs and conditions of all board members. Maintaining professionalism, however, must not equate to losing a sense of humor because meetings always present opportunities for laughter and fun. The key here is to eliminate comments that could be seemingly harmless to you but potentially demeaning or derogatory to everyone else. Real-life examples of cases in which improper humor caused offense and strained relationships are listed below.

- One CEO encountered problems with his board when he invited a well-known planning consultant to present a proposal to the board. During the course of the presentation, the consultant joked and used the terms "lettuce and tomatoes" and "salad dressing" as a comparison to his firm's proposed pricing strategy for the organization's mammography services and full OB/GYN product line. One board member had just had a mastectomy and took great offense to the light-hearted presentation. Likewise, several other members did not like that the pricing strategy was presented in a "humorous" way. In the end, the consultant and his firm lost the job even though the CEO wanted to award the work to the firm. Worse yet, the CEO lost a great deal of credibility with the board.
- A human resources consultant was presenting to the board an update on labor issues when he made some seemingly innocent jokes about unions. The remark offended two members of the board. One member was related to a union leader and the other had a very good company-union relationship and felt that putting unions down was totally inappropriate.
- A marketing consultant lost a contract when she made a mistake of injecting her presentation with "doctor" jokes

and directly stating: "Take docs by the hand and lead them." Of course, the physician board members did not find the consultant's humor funny.

Do not hire board members' relatives. Nepotism or variations of it is often not a good business practice because too many possible problems, particularly ethical, can develop including charges of favoritism and the uneasiness of needing to terminate if the person is not suited for the position. Of course, several mitigating factors must be considered. First, a long organizational history of this hiring practice may exist, so you may not be able to end it abruptly, if at all. Second, the organization may be located in a community where hiring relatives may be an expectation; this reality is faced by many organizations, especially in rural areas. Third, the organization may be in a small community where the only qualified person is a board relative, which eliminates the need to recruit. In small communities, furthermore, seasonal or temporary positions possibly could be filled with children or younger relatives of the board members. Although hiring relatives on a short-term basis should be done with great caution, it may be one way to satisfy board members without creating problematic cases.

Working with boards is often an art rather than a science. The art involved usually requires the application of common sense. Each and every board member must be shown the utmost of respect. Planning encounters and programs with the board well in advance can be helpful because many problems are the result of poor or incomplete planning. Carefully consider the little problems as well as the bigger ones so that they do not add up.

Chapter Nine

HUMAN RESOURCES

Ethical conduct cannot always be legislated by management. Sometimes it must be forged in the resolution of conflicts over actual problems. What due process does is allow such questions to be aired and debated in a neutral corner. It succeeds where a code or policy guidebook may fail because it allows situations that cannot be anticipated to become part of the webbing of rules and standards by which employees are bound.

David Ewing in *Justice on the Job: Restructuring Grievances in the Nonunion Workplace* (1989)

ETHICS IN THE workplace has multiple implications for the organization, the community it serves, and the world. However, what has long been overlooked is the ethical implication of the human resources decisions made by executives. Although seemingly dramatic, the truth is executives are responsible for their employees' livelihood. Therefore, every human resources decision that executives make directly affects employees—either creating or relieving enormous burden. The following questions the ethical appropriateness of some human resources decisions.

79

- Should termination from a position for inability to perform the job's duties be treated any differently than termination for insubordination? *Unfortunately, many executives consider only the legal ramifications and not the ethical causes of terminations.*
- When an employee has a personality clash with a supervisor, when is the appropriate, and ethical, time for the supervisor to ask the employee to find another job? *In most organizations, the supervisor almost always gains the support of the executives. The manner in which executives deal with this issue presents ethical challenges for them.*
- To what extent is it appropriate for a supervisor to dictate an employee's outside activities (social, civic, political)? How can a supervisor determine whether these outside activities have a negative effect on the organization? *The higher the position of an employee, the greater the potential for her/him to affect the organization with her/his outside involvement. For example, what would be the ethical implications of promoting a Caucasian manager who belongs to an all-white country club?*
- A competent administrative assistant who had been with the organization for 21 years was laid off because the wife of the CEO did not like her. *Often, the administrative assistants who serve in executive offices have the least job security among all the employees in the organization. Moreover, they are also often asked to perform duties that may be inappropriate, such as running personal errands for the spouse of the CEO.*

In the confines of the executive suite, unethical actions might go unseen. However, outside the lofty offices, employees watch and remember all executive decisions, whether they pertain to them directly or not. Subsequently, they also witness ethical and unethical behavior and practices, which could damage the trust that they generally reserve for their executives. This chapter proposes guidelines on strengthening your ethical decision-making processes. Before reading the following protocols, please read—and preferably complete—the human resources ethics questionnaire (see Appendix A). The questionnaire is designed to assess your personal response to various human resources situations.

Be sensitive to religious affiliations. Many healthcare organizations have religious affiliations, which provide, and sometimes dictate, the context for their decision making. The religious tenet of almost every denomination emphasizes a simple truth: Every human being has dignity and worth. Therefore, regardless of the differences in affiliation between the organization and employee, all decisions must be sensitive to the dictate of the human law.

Practice the golden rule. Many executives have a mental picture of how they hope they will be treated if they are terminated. Unfortunately, for many other executives the mental picture stays on the mind because in reality many of them are dismissed without, or little, warning and with nothing to fall back on. Executives, whether or not they have had this experience, must approach human resources decision making with compassion and empathy. They should be respectful of the power and authority inherent in their position when making staff decisions.

Practice the corporate philosophy. Almost all organizations maintain that employees are their greatest resource. Therefore, all executives must consider to what extent this belief is evident in their human resources decisions and make changes when necessary.

Know human resources laws. Although following the law does not always mean being ethical, knowing the law implies the correct ethical spirit. Laws frequently represent the intent of society to be ethical and can provide excellent direction in decision making. Executives should consider both the spirit and intent behind the laws.

Evaluate the end result first. This protocol addresses the struggle between the needs of the organization and the needs of the employee. Many decisions that involve employees are made because of a supervisor's power or ego and result in no organizational or individual good, except for the supervisor. If no good will result from the decision and no one will benefit, the decision should not stand.

Evaluate who will benefit the most. Consider how best to maintain a balance between what is good for and needed by the employee and what is good for and needed by the organization. Evaluating and balancing these benefits are further complicated when the needs of the organization are actually created or dictated by the needs of the chief executives.

Develop a rationale for all personnel policies. All personnel policies and procedures should have a well-established and well thought-out rationale. The rationale should be clearly stated with the policy and should set the guidelines under which the policy is enforced.

Establish a system of due process for employees. A system of due process provides an opportunity for employees to question the decisions of the organization and ensures that justice will prevail as much as possible. Due process at its base level is an organizational system for resolving complaints and conflict. It is more than simply a grievance procedure; it is a corporate attitude that shows that the organization has a sincere interest in its employees and their concerns. Managers should not view due process as a win-or-lose system.

Corporate due process is spreading in the United States. A book by David W. Ewing, *Justice on the Job: Resolving Grievances in the Nonunion Workplace,* reviews the system of due process at several leading U.S. corporations. He notes that these programs emphasize the process, not the answers. The process must have integrity and credibility, and employees must be free to use it and must ultimately believe that it can work for them.

Develop a human resources philosophy. Executives should develop and live by a philosophy or value statement, on both corporate and individual levels, that outlines how employees will be treated in the organization. Figure 9.1 is an example of a human resources corporate philosophy statement.

Consider the effects of all decisions, especially when the decision is a termination. Obviously, if the decision involves termination, which some have coined as "economic capital punishment," at least one person involved is hurt. Although some employees report of feeling better, or relieved, after being let go, the process is disheartening for everyone involved. Many organizations have a rule of not terminating any employee without the approval of either the chief human resources officer, the CEO, or both. This system of checks and balances helps to ensure fairness and ethical approach and gives someone other than the immediate supervisor a chance to review the circumstances and the facts of each case. Ideally, the fairness of termination decisions will improve as a result, and the ethical dimensions will be considered. The following are protocols for ethical, and legal, termination.

- *Be prepared to be challenged.* Be certain that the decision to terminate is truly necessary and final, but be prepared to respond to information presented by the employee. Assemble as many facts and as much evidence as possible and consider the potential for legal or other challenges. However, if the employee presents enough convincing information that could alter your decision, be prepared to hold your final decision. If necessary, executives should

83

Figure 9.1: Human Resources Philosophy of Employees of ABC Healthcare

We believe there is a direct connection between the quality of care that our patients receive and the positive spirit and morale that our staff feels. In short, a satisfied staff is dedicated to helping patients become satisfied. To that end, our human resources philosophy is geared toward the following:

- All staff (employees, physicians, volunteers) deserve to be treated with dignity. This means that interpersonal interactions should be handled with respect and courtesy.
- When rules and policies are necessary within our organization, all staff members deserve to be given a reason for them.
- A due process procedure will be used to provide all staff with the chance to challenge events that affect them.
- Secrets can be detrimental to the trust within our organization. We will strive to develop and maintain open communications and honesty in our dealings with one another.
- We will strive to build accountability into our structures, policies, and management.
- We will strive to create an environment where positive attitudes are recognized and rewarded, where diversity is valued and respected, where people value and respect the role of all staff, and where we recognize that no one person can do it all.

tell the employee that the new facts need to be reviewed and a new meeting will be scheduled soon. Soon must mean soon. Do not become preoccupied with other business and fail to follow through. Avoid having employees sit at home waiting as you gather, consider, or investigate information.

- *Follow the proper procedures.* The method of termination should be preestablished and consistent across the organization, even for higher-level positions.

- *Be prepared for any reaction.* Executives should seriously consider the employee's reaction and should anticipate needs, wants, or demands. Seemingly unimportant details must be taken care of such as making available a supply of tissues.
- *Do it yourself.* Although another executive or a human resources personnel could be invited to the conference, the direct supervisor is responsible for delivering the termination.
- *Consider the timing.* Both the time of day and the day of the week are important in scheduling a termination meeting. For example, if the termination took place in the middle of the day, the following questions should be considered:

1. Will the employee need to finish her/his shift or go back to the work area?
2. Should the employee be accompanied afterward to ensure she/he does not do anything inappropriate to office property?
3. Should any office documents, equipment, or supply taken by the employee be listed and approved?
4. Will other employees, possibly friends, be there? If so, should they see or talk to the terminated employee afterward?

Before allowing the terminated employee a number of days or even weeks to finalize projects, executives should carefully consider whether doing so would provide the possibly bitter employee an opportunity to bring down staff morale or sabotage equipment, current projects, or client contacts.

Most outplacement consultants maintain that the worst time to terminate a person is on Friday because the next day is Saturday, which is a non-work day so it (1) prevents the terminated employee from contacting business associates with whom she/

he might discuss job options or possible career leads; and (2) provides the employee an opportunity to brood and become more upset.

- *Be on time.* Do not make the employee wait and prolong anxiety. This is not the time to have a previous meeting run long or to squeeze in a few more return phone calls. In fact, allowing some private time to prepare is wise.
- *Get to the point quickly.* A termination meeting is not the time for friendly, extraneous conversation about families or the weather. Although you should not "fire the bullet" as soon as the employee enters the room, you should focus on the issue and move on.

  If the termination is unexpected, executives should be prepared for argument, debate, denial, and pleas for another chance. They should be humane and allow some of this conversation to occur; however, they should maintain control of the meeting. As Michael Covert says: "If firing has to be done, do it; but do it with style and treat the person(s) right."

SPECIFIC PROTOCOLS FOR DISMISSING MANAGERS

- *Give Appropriate Warnings.* Do not dismiss a manager immediately. She/he should have been involved in frank discussions that clearly delineated shortcomings and expectations.

  Executives should determine who, for practical or political reasons, needs to know about the termination in advance. Although confidentiality is paramount in any termination cases, some board members or key physicians may consider it an affront if they are not notified in advance of certain terminations.
- *Consider legal ramifications.* Some executives routinely discuss terminations with outside legal counsel before

proceeding. Executives should not be caught during the termination without all of the pertinent facts. Therefore, they must review initial letters of employment offer and contracts to ascertain that the organization has provided the terms of the agreement during the manager's tenure. In addition, executives must also: (1) present the employee with all of the legally required benefit information or options available; (2) anticipate any questions about salary continuance and benefits; and (3) clearly spell out alternatives in case they are warranted.

Many attorneys have standard agreement forms available that cover most termination contingencies. If such forms are used, the manager being terminated should be given one. Often the termination/severance agreement includes provisions whereby the employee waives the right to sue. If this is the case, be certain that the agreement is reviewed beforehand by a competent labor attorney.

- *Prepare for an announcement.* When a manager is dismissed, a discussion with her/him about the announcement of the dismissal is appropriate. For the manager's immediate staff, a private announcement is necessary. For the rest of the organization, or for the public, a news or press release is in order.
- *Discuss the transition.* The executive and the terminated manager should make plans for handling unfinished projects to ensure an orderly shift of responsibilities.
- *Be considerate of the terminated manager's support staff.* Administrative assistants or support staff often have strong allegiances to their immediate supervisors. They may be especially upset about the termination and may have some difficulty making the transition to a new supervisor.
- *Use outplacement firms.* Executives should take care to choose a reputable firm who will work with the dismissed

employee. In selecting an outplacement firm, make sure that it:

1. does not use expect the terminated employee to pay all or part of the fee. Reputable outplacement firms work only with clients whose former employer pays the entire fee;
2. provides full assessment services and not simply office and telephone backup;
3. has a good track record of placing clients in new positions;
4. offers privacy and dignified surroundings to the dismissed employee;
5. provides ongoing counseling and support;
6. provides basic tools and amenities such as out-of-town newspapers, fax machines, copy machines, industry guides, and professional journals and circulars; and
7. employs counselors who care and are concerned about for the well-being of the dismissed employees.

REFERENCE

Ewing, D. 1989. *Justice on the Job: Restructuring Grievances in the Nonunion Workplace.* Boston: Harvard Business School Press.

Chapter Ten

WRITTEN AND VERBAL COMMUNICATION

Whether you are an established or developing leader, you must cope with situations and circumstances you did not create, and over which you might think you have little control. However, there is one thing over which you do have total control—the way you speak and listen.

Kim Krisco in *Leadership and the Art of Conversation* (1997)

EXECUTIVES WHO LACK proper communication skills are poor leaders because communication is the medium through which leaders can demonstrate competency in all four factors of the executive excellence equation. This chapter catalogs the protocols for enhancing interaction whether it occurs informally in the hallway, formally in a board meeting, in person, or on paper.

VERBAL COMMUNICATION

Because verbal communication reveals the speakers' immediate emotional response—passion, anger, stress, concern, or excitement—in an unfettered, personal way, its impact is more observable, memorable, and even influential. Informal day-to-day interaction, including nonverbal communication and formal speeches or presentations, are ways we relate to others. The following are protocols for proper verbal communication in both informal and formal settings.

DAY-TO-DAY   INTERACTION

Practice dialogue, not monologue. Getting a point across hinges on a two-way interaction, especially when an order or instruction is being given. Exchange and feedback are important in ensuring that both parties understand and agree with each other. Too often, however, executives do not give others a chance to respond to their verbal messages mostly because of time constraints brought on by busy schedules. Subordinates, in turn, get too intimidated to ask for clarification and, hence, interpret the message incorrectly. There are four ways to improve dialogue between executives and staff.

1. Pause frequently to give staff the opportunity to ask clarifying questions.
2. Avoid seeming rushed when giving directions.
3. Ask staff to repeat the instructions to ensure understanding.
4. Go back to staff later to ostensibly check on progress but covertly clarify the initial instructions, if necessary.

One-on-one communication rarely takes place in group meetings because of the limited time available and the impersonal atmosphere. (Certain types of communication are too personal and private to be discussed in a group setting, despite the closeness of the group). However, executives must still dialogue with the group and welcome feedback from individual members; they should: (1) keep messages simple, (2) repeat main points several times, (3) allow plenty of time for questions and answers, and (4) follow up with a written summary.

Establish the practice of "Friday Issues." To establish an informal, routine form of communication, executives may find useful asking each subordinate to prepare a weekly list—consisting of three to four issues—of problems that each has encountered during the week. Some executives call these "Friday Issues" because these lists are often prepared on Friday for the executive to review over the weekend. Friday issues need not be formal; a short handwritten summary of key weekly issues will suffice.

Learn to disarm. Disarming is the technique of being the first to speak up about a negative issue that is expected to be raised. By disarming, the executive can be proactive rather than reactive and defensive. In addition, adversaries lose the element of surprise when the other party is first to raise the problem and immediately proposes points of compromise or solution. Executives should not wait for others to raise their negative issues. If no solutions or room for compromises are available, the executive should state this and the reasons for it early.

Disarming particularly works well in group situations. If someone within a group is expected to bring up a tough question or point, leaders may wish to do so first to retain control of the audience and to maintain poise—responding defensively to negative inquiries, particularly if no solutions can satisfy the group, is especially difficult.

Be aware of nonverbal messages. Executives should manage their nonverbal communication as carefully as they manage their words. The following are examples of seemingly innocent actions that could be misinterpreted.

- Staying behind the desk instead of coming around to meet someone;
- Dropping in unannounced on other managers to discuss issues instead of summoning them to the office;

- Keeping a suit jacket on instead of taking it off; and
- Sitting at the head of the conference room table or choosing to sit with or far away from someone. One successful nursing executive admits to choosing to sit beside a group member with whom she expects to disagree. Her logic is that the physical proximity of the other member would make confrontation, attacks, or challenges to her opinion difficult to mete out.

Eye contact, facial expressions, and body language also indicate a person's implicit mindset. Eye contact and facial expressions reveal interest or distraction, emotion or lack of it, and attention or disregard. Executives should always maintain good eye contact and provide nonverbal feedback to speakers, indicating through facial expressions that you heard and understood them. Body language also reveals true responses. For example, openness is signified by leaning toward a person or keeping the arms on the side of the body, while defensiveness or anger is shown by folding the arms or moving away from a person. The distance that people maintain can also be interpreted as signifying either friendliness or aloofness. Executives should not penetrate another person's space because doing so could be misinterpreted negatively and inappropriately. A person's body language cannot always be read accurately. In fact, some people will consciously use their body language to confuse, while others will simply contort their body unknowingly. No matter the intent, executives must be aware that every action has either a conscious or subconscious meaning.

Listen. You become a better communicator and better doer when you listen. Listen for:

- the meaning behind what is being said, and interpret and clarify, if necessary;

- areas of personal interest so you can relate without inserting your own bias and prejudice, which could influence the speaker; and
- the verbal and nonverbal message. Consider the message holistically not as part of a whole.

SPEECHES AND PRESENTATIONS

Presentations and speeches are formal, planned communications. The following protocols can be helpful in making effective speeches and presentations.

Prepare, prepare, prepare. Preparation must be done internally and externally. Internal preparation demands from the speaker knowledge of the specific material and overall subject area. External preparation refers to handling of mundane details such as room location and condition, audiovisuals, and handouts. Thoroughly studying, repeatedly rehearsing in front of an audience, and timing the presentation are the best way to prepare internally. Often, the most persuasive, educational, smooth-flowing, and easy to follow presentations are delivered from the heart rather than the mind. This means that the speaker learned the material so well that she/he does not need to refer to any notes or outlines. The audiences at these presentations are so captured that they participate in exercises, ask questions, and respond as if they are having an informal, one-on-one conversation with the speaker. Presentations about legal issues, however, must usually follow an absolute script because deviating from specific preselected words and phrases or leaving out important terms can skew the entire presentation and its goal.

External preparation is sometimes more difficult to choreograph because a lot of factors beyond the presenter's control are at play. Therefore, the presenter must have a contingency plan if any of the following occurs.

- The projector breaks and you cannot show your overheads.
- You bring ten sets of handouts and twenty people show up.
- Your overheads are too small to be read by people in the back of the room.
- You lose your notes.
- You are in a room that is much too hot or cold. The meeting room has only one door and it is located at the front of the room, and you expect people to arrive late or leave early.
- The key decision maker of the group to which you are making a presentation is not in the meeting.
- Your presentation relies heavily on a videotape and the tape or the video player gets damaged.
- Your computer is not compatible with the screen projector.

When the presentation will be given in an unfamiliar room, executives should try to visit it ahead of time to get a feel for the space and ascertain its needs and challenges. Equipment should also be tested out.

Do not apologize. Any form of apology will allow some members of the audience to immediately tune a speaker out. Speakers should never apologize for:

- their presence if they were a replacement. They should act as if they were the originally scheduled speaker;
- a cold or an ailment; and
- not being prepared.

WRITTEN COMMUNICATION

Although verbal communication is more effective on a short-term basis, written communication is more significant on a long-term basis because it is recorded and unequivocal and can be reviewed and interpreted repeatedly. Therefore, it is more risky.

The protocols that follow can help executives communicate more effectively in writing.

Develop a mental checklist. Before writing, executives should think of a checklist of questions to determine why they are writing, for whom they are writing, and in what format they are writing—memo, letter, or informal note. E-mail has become the quickest, if not the most utilized, way of corresponding. However, executives must be aware that e-mails do not have the same confidential safeguards as other traditional formats do, so caution must also be used when sending or receiving a message.

Consider your timing. Often, the timing of a note, memo, or letter is more important than the content. Executives should try to determine the best time to send correspondence. Writing when upset or angry is not advisable because, although emotions are fleeting, the written words describing the emotions are not. If a correspondence must be written, repeated reading of the content is necessary to avoid later embarrassment or retraction. Sending e-mail responses late at night when one is tired, or without careful attention and reflection to the message, may also cause problems.

Written communication should be avoided when verbal interaction would suffice. If the issue is personal in nature, a face-to-face encounter is usually better, even when executives cannot find time to do so. Ideally, executives should respond to all written correspondence addressed to them. One hospital CEO answered every piece of mail within 24 hours. Even though much of that mail asked for information or decisions that would take additional time to research, this executive sent an acknowledgment letter to the sender, which indicated an approximate time when the sender could expect further response.

Use your own supplies. Corporate letterhead must be used strictly for corporate matters only. Executives should use personal stationery and their own supply of stamps for personal correspondence they write at the office. This protocol is often violated when executive job seekers print their cover letters and resumes on organizational paper and envelope. Even if the job seeker's present employer does not object to this practice, it may raise questions in the minds of recipients about the applicant's sense of propriety.

Decide who should receive copies. Executives must carefully consider who to give copies of correspondence on a case-by-case basis. As a general guideline, one's superior should receive copies in any pertinent situation to avoid surprises.

Use a clear writing style. Executives should not use jargon or pedantic language. They should write clearly and succinctly. Executives must target their writing to the knowledge and level of interest of their recipients. Write clearly with the following tips.

- *Use concrete language.* For example, "We had a 10 percent nosocomial infection rate" is preferable to "Our infection rate was high last year."
- *Specify action with simple, recognizable terminology and phrases.* For example, "stop" is preferable to "cease and desist"; "Terminate the employee" is clearer than "Give due consideration and reflection to ending the employment relationship of the employee."
- *Be direct.* For example, "Meet with me no later than next week to conclude our decision on the matter" is better than "Let us get together next week to make our final decision."

Develop a consistent style. One of the marks of professionalism is consistency. Therefore, in building an image, executives must use a consistent writing style to symbolize their personal distinguishing mark. Executives may want to consider using a middle initial, spelling out all abbreviations, or not using contractions in all correspondence.

Get the facts before writing. When facts are written, they can easily be tested. Although a wrong fact or figure may stand in verbal presentations, they are inappropriate in written materials because they mislead and could destroy the credibility of the message and presenter.

Send handwritten notes. Handwritten notes are appropriate on certain occasions. They send a strong personal signal that executives have taken extra time to consider the content of their correspondence. A tragic loss or misfortune is one of the occasions in which sending a handwritten note is appropriate. In these situations, a brief note that offers assistance and sympathy can mean a lot to the recipient. Although an e-mail on various matters may be appreciated, personal handwritten notes send a message of style and class.

Chapter Eleven

PHYSICIAN RELATIONSHIPS

If physicians are represented on the board, if they sit on the major committees and management sits on theirs, if management is open to physician influence and accessible, in short, if they are involved, then physicians usually feel positive about the appropriateness and extent of their voice.

Alan Sheldon in *Managing Doctors* (1986)

T O THE PUBLIC, physicians are the most-recognized representation of the healthcare industry. Not only are physicians gatekeepers of healthcare access in that they introduce millions of patients to healthcare services and, hence, generate exorbitant income for the industry; they are also the industry's most demanding customers and, hence, are its most influential, if not vocal, change agents. Physician influence, therefore, is always present and often desired in healthcare organizations. Executives who want to gain support for their policies and change proposals must cultivate a positive working and interpersonal relationship with physicians. This relationship will not only establish a network for the executive but will also strengthen the union between physicians and the organization. Regardless of the financial and systematic rewards of establishing good relationships with physicians, executives must bestow them the respect they deserve for their life-enhancing contributions to society. Despite the necessity of developing a good relationship with physicians, however, many executives harbor negative feelings and view working with physicians as the most difficult part of their jobs. Some executives cease trying because they believe that most physicians are so intent on their own agendas and concerns that they cannot be open minded about administrative restrictions. This mindset is not only inappropriate, it also encourages conflict and guarantees failure at establishing a good relationship. If given appropriate information and explanation, physicians can and do work well with executives. Although executives should not pay physicians more respect than what is paid to other healthcare providers, give them preferential treatment, excuse inappropriate conduct, or be fearful and intimidated, they should consider the ongoing rigors of physician life, including the following, to understand their thought processes.

- New physicians and medical students typically work 90 to 100 hours per week, which drastically limit the time they spend with family and friends.
- Physicians face constant ethical and life-and-death dilemmas.
- Physicians work everyday under extreme pressure from patients who count on them to deliver total satisfaction — a cure — and who, naturally, have no tolerance for error.
- Physicians' mistakes can be fatal, figuratively and literally.
- Physicians are personally liable for professional mishaps.

Developing a good relationship is a mutual collaboration between two parties in that both parties must be willing to respect, understand, and learn from each other. But what happens when mutual dislike and distrust are at play — as is generally the case between physicians and executives? Because this book focuses only on executive excellence, the protocols in this chapter are intended to enhance the executive's understanding, hence respect, of physicians as customers and as business partners. This understanding is vital in establishing relationships.

PHYSICIANS AS CUSTOMERS

Executives must realize that admitting physicians are customers who expect to be provided with what they need and want. To remain competitive, executives must be informed of what other organizations offer their medical staff and provide comparable services and benefits. Executives should give physicians up-to-date, clear, concise information about their organization and remember that the physicians' needs and wants are not always related to new equipment or perfect working conditions. Instead, physicians are often interested in the strategic direction of the organization or in a particular area that could be changed.

Accommodate the physician's schedule. Executives should remember that may physicians earn their own income and are, therefore, in charge of their own work hours. Therefore, when scheduling meetings that necessitate involvement of physicians, executives must make certain that the meetings are scheduled to be convenient for the physician, start and end on time, and are efficiently managed.

Accept that physicians are patient advocates. Because of the physician's obligation to care for and assist the patient, physicians and patients develop relationships. This relationship often translates to patient advocacy. Generally, executives are uncomfortable with advocacy of any kind because it often pushes causes and issues that may not be practical or attainable for the organization.

Give reasons and explanations. Physicians are fact driven. They are trained to question every piece of information, so executives must be prepared to offer a well thought-out explanation for every decision, policy, process, or change made. Executives must note that physician questioning is not done to challenge authority but to fully understand issues that affect their practice.

Don't play favorites. Fairness can be a problematic issue in organizations with a large number of hospital-based physicians. In these organizations, community-based physicians frequently feel like second-class citizens because hospital-based physicians often have better access to information and more frequent access to hospital executives. Executives should exercise extra care to avoid the perception that hospital-based doctors are given preference because showing favoritism usually harms all past efforts toward working with the medical staff. Physicians who split their patient admissions among hospitals should not be undermined because if treated properly these physicians could increase their admissions for the organization.

Establish a procedural justice system. Procedural justice system allows individuals to question, and challenge, the rationale behind actions that affect them. Ideally, healthcare organizations should establish a similar system of appeal for its stakeholders — the physicians — so that they can effectively understand administrative issues such as construction of physician facilities, purchase of capital equipment, request for medical record support, etc. The procedural justice system maybe informal where executives may just need to show an open willingness to hear medical staff concerns and explain the rationale for their decisions. Most physicians recognize that the procedural justice system does not always produce satisfactory or desired outcome, but they do expect to receive a reasonable explanation.

Share information. Physician leadership should be kept apprised of events and plans because many of them are members of the medical executive committee, department heads, or informal leaders among the medical staff. Regardless of their status within the organization, all physicians should be involved in the strategic planning process in a real and continuous way. Although written communication is not always the most practical way of sharing information, a well-written and frequently published physician newsletter is a good tool. Routine telephone calls by executives are an effective method for staying in touch. Many CEOs and executives make a practice of touching base with physicians over breakfast meetings, while some executives share and discuss ideas in more informal settings such as the golf course or fitness club.

Avoid making clinical decisions. Clearly, executives should not intervene in or address clinical decisions but must defer the decision to, or at least consult with, physicians. If at all feasible, executives should approach a full-time physician executive on staff to fully handle the situation.

Hire or maintain a physician relations liaison. All, but the smallest, hospitals should be able to afford employing a physician relations liaison. The physician relations liaison focuses on the physicians' office staff. The primary job of the physician liaison is the identification, and early alleviation, of small issues that often burgeon into major sources of dissatisfaction for the medical staff. The liaison must have access to the organization's decision makers and should be available to the physicians' office staff on a routine basis.

Survey physicians. Surveying, either through written or focus group means, physicians on a regular basis to determine their concerns and interests is paramount to improving physician satisfaction and enhancing relationships. Once identified, executives should address the issues put forth as soon as is practical.

Respond quickly and follow up. Not all requests or questions that executives receive from physicians are easy or have straightforward answers. However, whether the answer is vague, negative, or complicated, executives must practice the act of responding quickly. Neglecting to respond quickly decreases the executive's credibility with the physician. Following up after a response is given must also be practiced because the executive must determine if the response is satisfactory or lacking.

Involve physicians' support staff in organizational activities. Physicians' support staff should be included in organization-sponsored educational programs and mailings because most physicians utilize their staff to an even greater degree than other professionals do and give them much more latitude and autonomy for decision making. The support staffs often act as an extension of the physician and often influence admitting decisions if the doctor belongs to the admitting staff of more than one hospital. Executives must realize that paying attention to the physician while ignoring the support staff results in losing the physician.

Involve physicians in strategic planning. Because physicians must work in such a fast-paced manner, their day-to-day tasks and decision-making processes must be performed rapidly as well. Physicians' patient advocacy role also makes long waits for solutions intolerable. Therefore, physicians often are not accustomed to, get impatient with, and do not understand the drawn-out decision making and implementation processes that last for many months or even years. In light of this, executives should involve physicians in long-term strategic planning to make them understand the process and appreciate the careful, if bureaucratic, process.

Be a doer. Physicians respect doers. Therefore, executives must constantly deliver on promises and must consistently act rather than constantly say.

PHYSICIANS AS BUSINESS PARTNERS

Healthcare organizations and physicians continue to partner with each other. Although some of these partnerships have been successful, most have been failures. Recent partnerships have often involved employment relationships, which usually initiate the conflict in ventures. In some instances, these failures stem from personal conflicts between the partners, while in others, they result from economic models that could not work. The protocols below prescribe a new mindset for executives when dealing with physician partners. These protocols intend to ease tensions between partners.

Consider risk differences. Executives represent healthcare organizations that have imposing resources and a great deal of capital backing. Therefore, executives likely do not have personal stakes in the organization's business dealing or its subsequent failure or success, so their risks are low, if nonexistent. To executives, a business transaction is only one of the many organizational realities that they encounter on a regular basis. On the other hand, physicians enter into contracts and agreements as individuals, not as representatives as executives do. The physician's business is personal because its success and failure are dependent on the physician's skills and training. Therefore, physicians operate at high risks. To them, the business deal is everything—personal, professional, and financial. This mindset is true for most physicians even in employment relationships, however.

Consider portability issues. Many physicians perceive executives as frequent job changers because most physicians go through frequent leadership changes within their organizations; hence, they have developed a perception that executives are not committed to long-term assignments or partnerships. In contrast, a physician's practice cannot easily, or feasibly, be transferred. Typically, physicians remain in one location their entire professional life.

Consider generational work values. Physicians' business values depend on three factors: (1) stage in their medical careers, (2) location of practice, and (3) type of specialty. These factors, and variations thereof, strongly affect how physicians practice medicine and how they form relationships with healthcare organizations. New physicians who started their medical practice only in the last few years and veteran physicians who have been practicing for several decades differ greatly.

Reasons of this difference include, but are not limited to, the evolution of various reimbursement systems, technology, and the rise of a younger, diverse generation of professionals who espouse different work ethics. For example, recent medical school graduates are likely to be female, to come from a wide range of socioeconomic groups, to have studied medical ethics and business office management, to not be natives of the community in which they practice, to be more geographically mobile, to be willing to work on a salaried basis, and to not set up solo practices. In contrast, veteran physicians are likely to be more loyal to organizations and to have strong ties to the communities in which they practice because they are likely to have grown up or at least spent many years there.

Consider ramifications of practice location. Hospital-based physicians tend to be pathologists, radiologists, anesthesiologists, and emergency care specialists. Although these physicians may have outside offices, they conduct the bulk of their administrative duties and perform medical services in the hospital, which is the opposite practice for physicians with private practices outside of the hospital. Generally, hospital-based physicians are more attached to the hospital and frequently interact with managers, executives, and leaders of the organization.

Consider needs. Because executives and hospital-based physicians see each other more — hence, know each other better — they view them as insiders and tend to treat them more informally than they do doctors who maintain outside offices and admit patients to other hospitals. As a result, hospital-based physicians may feel taken for granted and not paid attention to. Further, hospital-based physicians have little opportunity to meet their needs outside the organization, so they need to be assured that the organization with which they partner attempts to meet, or at least negotiate, demands; ensures fair appropriations of resources; and is willing to involve them in organizational processes, such as budgeting. Involving hospital-based physicians in the budgeting process must entail more than merely informing them of budget decisions, executives must solicit and consider physicians' requests and input and must respond to them on a personal basis.

Consider specialties. Often, medical specialties dictate physician behavior because these specialties also train them how to respond. For example, surgeons usually are involved in comparatively brief interventions. Executives should keep in mind that surgeons are action oriented so they seek to diagnose the causes of and solutions to problems with expediency. Surgeons tend to be comfortable with technology and focused on the capital processes of the organization. In contrast, family practitioners are people oriented and are comfortable with processes. They focus on issues and are trained to be good listeners.

Executives should never approach physicians in the same manner because, as I have laid out, physician behavior, mindset, and work ethic vary greatly and depend on multiple factors. Executives should get to know the physicians with whom the organization partners by meeting with them either formally or informally. The best way to learn more about the organization's community-based physicians who have off-site practices is to visit them at their offices. This method will not only communicate that the executive is interested in building a good relationship, it will also encourage trust between partners.

Chapter Twelve

RECRUITMENT AND SELECTION

Recruitment of high-level professionals in all industries has
always been based on relationship building.

Roger Bonds in *Physician Recruitment
and Retention* (1991)

A CHIEF EXECUTIVE OFFICER once told me: "I have
been in the field for 24 years and I have yet to go through
more than a six month period when I had an entire
management team in place. I have always been recruiting." Although this admission of the executive's staff-turnover battle can
be easily interpreted as a product of underdeveloped leadership
skills, it is not accurate or fair in this context because the executive was extremely competent, effective, and respected. So why
cannot the executive keep a management staff for long periods?
The answer may simply reflect the reality of turnover in the field;
however, it often lies in the strength or weakness of the organization's recruitment and selection process. The following are
hallmark, and real, cases of poor recruitment and selection.

Case 1: A candidate was set up for a day of interviewing with a
number of executives. The CEO, to whom the candidate was to
report, was scheduled for a two-hour breakfast meeting. Fifteen

minutes into their meeting, the CEO was paged and had to call the hospital. By the time he had finished with the crisis, he only had 30 minutes left to spend with the candidate. Neither the CEO nor the candidate could not make up the lost time later that day. Several weeks later, the search firm informed the candidate that another candidate had been selected for the position. The rejected candidate was convinced that a lack of time with the CEO was a key factor in not being selected for a follow-up interview.

Case 2: An Eastern health system, which hired a search firm to recruit a corporate vice president for its three hospitals, brought in the top three candidates recommended by the search consultant. A finalist was brought back for a second two-day visit and then invited back with his spouse for a third visit. During the third visit, the candidate and his wife spent two additional days meeting hospital staff and touring the area with a realtor. Three weeks after the third visit, the candidate still had not received a formal offer, but received a call from the search consultant who informed him that the organization had decided to restart the search from scratch because an internal struggle had occurred between the system CEO and the administrator of the flagship hospital. The leading candidate, although he met the qualifications required by the CEO, did not meet the criteria desired by the administrator of the flagship hospital.

Case 3: A competent vice president interviewed at a competing hospital for a lateral position. The initial interview with the hospital's COO took place in January and went so well that the candidate was informed that she was one of the strongest candidates and would definitely be included in the second round of interviews. In February, the candidate called the COO to check on the progress of the search. The COO expressed continued strong interest and, after a few days, scheduled the candidate for another round of interviews with seven executives over 15 different days. The candidate complied and came for all of the interviews. At this point, the confidentiality of her candidacy had been severely compromised. During each interview, the candidate was left on her own to find each office. For six of the seven interviews, the candidate waited at least ten minutes past the appointed time for the interview; one appointment began 40 minutes late.

In April, the COO informed the candidate that she was one of two finalists and would be scheduled for an interview with the hospital's consulting psychologist; the meeting with the psychologist was not scheduled until three weeks later. Although the candidate doubted the relevance of the psychologist's interview and the psychological tests she was given, she complied with the requirement. Three weeks later, the COO contacted the candidate to inform her that another candidate was chosen for the position. Later, the rejected candidate learned that the hospital hired an individual with no hospital experience. She concluded that CEO must have vetoed the COO's decision. The candidate felt that her time with the CEO had been rushed and that it was a contributing factor in the selection. Moreover, she highly resented the haphazard interview process that exposed her candidacy in her own organization.

Change is more frequently caused by staff turnover and vacancies than by any other factor because people are the ones who change the culture of an organization. With change comes stress. Executives must reverse this stress by carefully recruiting and selecting people who can affect this culture. This chapter focuses on the details that tend to get overlooked in the larger scheme of recruiting and selecting employees or members of the executive team. Recruiting thoughtfully, and with class, will not only distinguish your organization from others but will also help you assemble a stronger team.

Adhere to the agreed-upon schedule. Most executives allow daily activities to interrupt and interfere with the interview process.

As a result, many interviewees have experienced unpleasant and unnecessary last-minute schedule changes, late starts and/or late ends, or long waits before and between interviews. Although not all interviews can be perfectly orchestrated, because in health-care a lot of issues come up that do not and cannot yield to time limits or agendas, all interviews must be conducted with consideration for the interviewee's other time obligations.

Treat applicants as customers. Each interview is an opportunity for both candidate and interviewer to convince each other of what each can offer. Therefore, if you are the interviewer, your responsibility is to market your organization and its benefits so that the applicant, who obviously has something to offer otherwise she/he would not have made it as far as talking with you, would want to buy or at least consider it.

Add value to the recruitment process. Recruiting is, in essence, a courting process because you and your organization are competing against others to win the attention of the candidate. Consider some, or all, of the suggestions below to add value to your recruitment package.

- Pick up the candidate at the airport, if necessary. If not, at least ensure that the candidate receives directions.
- Information and insight about local real-estate markets and the communities surrounding the organization, in case the candidate decides to relocate, is appreciated.
- Make certain that the manager of the hotel where the candidate is staying knows that your candidate is a VIP guest, so that the staff can pay closer attention to the candidate's needs. Have the candidate's room and meal expenses billed directly to the organization. Check the room to ensure that it is equipped to meet comfort levels.
- By the second visit, a fruit basket or flowers waiting in the candidate's hotel room is a great welcoming touch.

- Careful attention to the spouse is often a critical determinant in the success or failure of recruitment.
- A carefully planned and appropriate realtor's tour is important in showing the best of the community.

Stick to the schedule. Arrive on time. Stick to the agenda. Avoid running long. Prevent, or at least minimize, the waiting time between interviews. If unavoidable interruptions come up, provide the candidate some appropriate reading material.

Honor confidentiality. Although some executives are relatively open to their staff considering other opportunities, most are not. Therefore, most candidates do not want their present employers aware of their interest in another position, so recruiters must make every effort to protect every candidate's confidentiality. Consider the following seemingly innocent confidentiality breaches.

- An executive on the interview team who knows another executive in the same town makes a "confidential" call and asks about the candidate.
- An executive calls someone who recently worked in the same organization.
- An executive from the interviewing organization calls a close colleague who works in the same organization as the candidate.

Confidentiality breaches, such as the examples given, occur quite frequently, especially in small industries like healthcare because of the large networks that executives form among each other. As illustrated by the examples, some executives do not view casual inquiries a problem; in fact, they reason that this is the risk that candidates run when they interview. This attitude is unfortunate and inappropriate. Once the process of checking references begins, interviewers must make certain that candidates understand, and at times permit, that people other than those listed on the official reference list may be called to provide background information.

Provide a realistic job preview. Research has shown that candidates who are given a complete — positive and negative — job preview are more likely to (1) remove themselves from contention if they deem the position unsuitable to their needs; (2) have a more reasonable and realistic set of expectations when they begin work; and (3) be less disappointed, angry, or dissatisfied if hired. Because many healthcare systems seem to be always hiring to replace employees or expand services, their recruiting practices almost always emphasizes the positive and leaves out the negative aspects of the organization and the position. Consider the following tactics to upsell. A vice president candidate is promised additional extra staffing support, although the promise is never precisely spelled out in a prehire letter.

Many organizations prefer to wait until very late in the interview process before discussing salary and benefits. Sometimes the reason behind deferring to discuss financial matters is simply that the organization cannot meet the candidate's requirement.

RECRUITING INTERNAL CANDIDATES

Although a number of healthcare organizations claim to have sophisticated succession planning programs, the overall industry record for promoting internally is weak. In fact, many executives find leaving their organizations necessary to advance their careers. Executives must keep in mind that sometimes the best candidates are the employees who are already on board because they not only have the skills or the foundation of knowledge required, they also already have insight on the organization, the job, and the culture within. Therefore, hiring internally is financially viable and practical for executives. The following are some general protocols for developing a solid policy on internal promotion or recruiting.

Carefully plan and time your response. Interviewers typically communicate very little to the internal candidate and often make the candidate wait a long time to update her/him on the status of the search. Internal candidates for executive positions sometimes receive their first notification that they are no longer being considered for a position on the same day they find out who had been hired. If internal candidates are not viable, let them know at the beginning of the process because having them wait is unethical and inhumane.

Do not give courtesy interviews. The interview process should be sincere and candid, and must not be used to appease employees who are not qualified but want to practice interviewing skills.

Do not use the internal candidate as a shill. Sometimes, internal candidates are cycled through an interview process only to make external candidates look stronger. Internal candidates see and know that they are being used for negative contrast.

Focus on the interview. When internal candidates come for their interviews, executives should interview them and not discuss organizational business. They should resist the temptation to conduct even a small amount of business or to deal with extraneous issues. Because executive search firms are now used widely by many healthcare organizations to relieve them of the stressful process of identifying suitable candidates, the following section delineates some of the general concepts, and financial aspects, of hiring and selecting executive search firms. Figure 12.1 details the reasons employers should consider using a search firm.

HIRING AN EXECUTIVE SEARCH FIRM

Exclusive, contingency, and fee-for-service are not only types of search firm services but also are types of fee arrangements. In an exclusive arrangement, or retained search, the employer typically

---

Figure 12.1: Reasons for Using a Search Firm

1. A search firm consultant provides traditional management consulting, such as advice on organizational needs and insight into what other similar organizations are doing and how to approach system issues.
2. Search firms help identify market salary ranges and peculiar aspects of a search that are not immediately apparent to the employer.
3. Many employers do not have the time or the expertise to handle executive searches. The search firm provides this needed expertise.
4. Sometimes, organizations need to begin searches confidentially to identify a candidate prior to the departure of the incumbent executive.
5. Many executives do not respond to, or are not aware of, newspaper or journal advertisements. They will more often respond to a search consultant's call.
6. A search firm casts a wider net for the identification of candidates.
7. Often, a search firm brings objectivity to the recruiting process. This objectivity is necessary when internal candidates are applying.

---

engages the services of one firm. The firm hired then performs all the recruiting functions including finding, assessing, and presenting qualified candidates. The employer pays the firm a set fee and reimburses additional expenses its consultants incur during the recruitment. This fee is due to the firm whether or not the employer finds a suitable candidate through the firm or on its own means. In a contingency search arrangement, the employer may engage several firms to identify one or more candidates. The professional fee is paid only if a firm-identified candidate is hired. In a fee-for-service arrangement, the employer employs a search firm to handle only parts of the recruiting functions such as screening candidates or checking references. The firm bills only for services it provided, whether or not it found a candidate.

Typically, search firms that only provide exclusive service work on behalf of the employer, while firms hired on a contingency basis tend to side with the candidates. In addition, some firms that only provide contingency searches have been known to make improper and misleading referrals. They often scour job-wanted postings in magazines and newspapers and present candidates to employers as perfect candidates with whom they have been working. Some of the consultants who work for these contingency firms also have never held positions in the industry, such as healthcare, in which they work. Once an employer decides to engage a firm, the simple protocols described below will help ensure a successful result.

Clearly express expectations and needs. Extensive and explicit discussion between the employer and the firm should take place before the search begins so that each party is aware of the parameters and permissible factors. This front-end preparation time is crucial in detailing goal expectations and specific competencies. Possible confusion about the search process should be managed as well. For example, the salary range of the position is $150,000–160,000, but could be increased to $175,000 if the most suitable candidate is found. The search consultant could misunderstand this range and inform the candidates that the position offers a starting salary of up to $175,000, which, of course, is false but very appealing.

Discuss recruitment procedures. Because the firm works for the employer, the employer has the right to know how each candidate will be treated and handled. If the firm is handling too many searches, candidates might not receive the best treatment, which could leave a bad impression that would reflect on the employer.

Stay connected and informed. Schedule routine progress evaluation and communication with the search consultant during the process. Anticipate problems to arise along the way and be prepared to handle them.

Involve the consultant in final salary negotiations. The consultant can be a helpful intermediary in the negotiation process because by the end of the search, both the candidate and the employer have developed a relationship with the consultant and are tendentious to be more open to the consultant than to each other. The employer must make certain, however, that parameters are well defined when the consultant is involved.

PROTOCOLS FOR CANDIDATES CONTACTED BY A SEARCH FIRM

Executives in the field should be prepared for calls from search consultants. They should take these calls whether or not they are interested in moving at the time. Building relationships with search consultants enhances a candidate's networking reach and often guarantees a call later in the future when a job move might be right. If uninterested in the opportunity presented, the candidate should try to provide two to three referrals to the consultant. Candidates must always be ready to sell themselves and be prepared for the search consultant to screen them during the conversation. When the call arrives, candidates should consider the following protocols.

Manage the length of each telephone conversation. A call from a firm may help the candidate's ego or may whet curiosity, but such calls, although are worthwhile, are time consuming. One way to regulate these calls is to keep a list of general questions or concerns; this list would help you guide, and focus, the conversation and stick to the schedule. If the candidate's time is limited to handle the call, setting an appointment for a later time is strongly advised.

Take notes. Write down as much detail as possible about the job and the employer during your conversation with the consultant or during your research. Being attentive to details and being knowledgeable are impressive qualities to consultants.

Ask for a job specification and salary range. Most search firms prepare extensive job specifications detailing the organization and the community, the position, its key goals, and the competencies/characteristics sought in the ideal candidate. Candidates should not hesitate to ask about salary or benefit expectations because these details have already been determined. Hesitating can only lead to wasted time for both you and the consultant.

GENERAL PROTOCOLS FOR CANDIDATES

Review and update resume. Colleagues and consultants are good reviewers because they would know what pertinent details employers, such as themselves, are looking for. Always keep it updated and ready to be mailed out.

Stay connected. Candidates and consultants should always take the time to contact each other, either to discuss the search or industry trends or simply swap ideas.

Make referrals. Candidates who were hired with the consultant's help, or at least identified for a position, can do the consultant a favor by referring him or her to other candidates or prospective candidates.

Be professional at interviews. Arrive on time; dress appropriately; bring additional copies of resume and an organizational chart that shows your most recent, or current, position; discuss specific measurable accomplishments; allow ample time in case it runs longer; discuss salary and relocation needs; and be prepared to express interest in the position, or lack of, soon after the interview.

INTERVIEW PROTOCOLS FOR CANDIDATES

Arrive early and tour the organization. Candidates might want to arrive the day before the interview and take a tour of the community and the organization's facilities. Talk with the staff and get a feel for the culture and mindset within the organization.

Ask for additional information and compare it with that given by the search consultant. Attempt to rectify any concerns or conflicts early in the process. Typically, the longer the discussions last between the candidate and the employer, the less likely they are to retract their positions.

Prepare for sensory overload. Overload often occurs if the candidate interviews with nine or ten people during the day. Remember that a candidate's enthusiasm, energy, and sales ability must remain sharp throughout the entire process.

Practice interview skills. Even when executives are not in the job market, they should test their qualifications against the current hiring practices occasionally (i.e., every two years or so). Interviewing practice not only hones the executive's ability to market her/his skills, but also helps her/him refocus goals and accomplishments.

Maintain a balance between listening and speaking. Without the proper amount of listening, learning about the position, the organization, and the executive to whom the candidate would report is impossible. On the other hand, if the candidate listens too much and does not speak enough, she/he may lose the interviewer's interest.

Be courteous to everyone. Candidates should be particularly courteous to staff—administrative assistants, administrative fellows and residents, etc.—who assist and escort them during the interview process. Many CEOs ask staff for their opinions of the candidates.

Chapter Thirteen

THE NEW POSITION

There are a lot of well-educated people in the white-collar world who are very smart about spreadsheets but don't know how to treat other people. And this isn't a matter of their not conforming to some pristine code of etiquette, but simply their having a frame of mind that is selfish and thoughtless.

Letitia Baldrige, renowned author and etiquette expert

T HE FIRST IMPRESSION lasts the longest so executives new to an organization must strive to set the appropriate tone immediately at the start of their tenure. During this initial period, a new executive's action and inaction and verbal and nonverbal communication are even more intensely watched. This chapter submits protocols for ensuring that the executive steps in with the "right foot."

Groom. Executives should pay special attention to dress, deportment, and hygiene. During the first few days, executives should wear "interview clothes" because a simple, classic outfit shows that the executive cares about looking good and about what other people think.

Be on time. Tardiness sends the wrong message to superiors and to subordinates. It intimates to subordinates that the executive feels so important that she/he (1) cannot be bothered with the menial task of abiding by a schedule, (2) must be waited on, and (3) does not value other people's time. To superiors, such as board members or chief executives, tardiness means that the executive is so disorganized that she/he cannot manage a schedule and is disrespectful of their time.

Be direct. When communicating or giving directives, new executives should be succinct without being abrupt. Vagueness would only imply that the executive is not strong enough for the leadership position and did not care about the outcomes of the order.

Spend time at the office. The amount of time a new executive spends on the job during the first several months communicates the degree of interest and loyalty. This time can be spent learning the organization's history, policies, services, culture, staff, and other nuances.

Articulate a personal philosophy. New executives should prepare their personal "philosophical statements," which communicate succinctly their management principles. These statements could include memorable themes and short phrases, and should be articulated frequently to staff during the first several weeks in a new position. Such interaction will help employees get to know the new executive and the managerial style and value system by which she/he abides. Articulating a managerial style through personal statements is tantamount to delivering a political pitch through a slogan, which is more memorable.

Be consistent. The fastest way that a new executive can establish credibility is through being consistent in moods, work habits, and interpersonal relationships. Consistent behavior makes people get comfortable with authority figures faster because they know what to expect.

Spell out expectations. New executives who are taking over an existing position and staff must spell out what they expect from their subordinates. Also, they must articulate the rationale behind their plans and directions, especially when new procedures are installed.

Be aware. Possessing an auditor's curiosity is a healthy characteristic for all executives; for new executives it is imperative. Regardless of the necessity of knowing and the disapproval of staff, executives must question all activities that flow through or around their areas of responsibility.

Listen and learn. Many staff members are very cooperative and are anxious to show and tell what they know if the new staff member is a willing listener, even if the new staff is an executive. In every organization, a new person must deal with the expectations of others. The process of exploring mutual expectations is vital during the initial few months on the job. Future changes should consider or include the wishes that staff may have articulated during the orientation process.

Deliberate but do not procrastinate. Although new executives can postpone making key decisions until they have learned enough about the organization, they cannot keep suspending their duty to rule.

Deliver on promises. Promises made during the first several weeks in a new position must be kept. Executives should keep a written record of any commitments made and check it against their accomplishments on a regular basis. Failing to follow through on promises leads to loss of credibility.

Use the "1-1-3-7" guide. 1-1-3-7 is a time frame that stands for first week, first month, third month, and seventh month on the job.

The time frame can guide a new executive through self-evaluation. Here's how it works:

- After the first week (1), the new executive should write a list of the five key problems within the organization and the five key movers and shakers with whom she/he will have to work to succeed. The purpose of the list is to record present reality and future changes and results. This list should be kept for personal perusal only and must be updated every few weeks.
- After the first month (1), the new executive should write a list of five to eight expectations for her/his first six months and five to eight very visible changes that could be made easily and quickly. These expectations should be generic statements of behavior or description of personal values, which can be easily verbalized to any group in the organization. One successful healthcare executive used phrases such as "organizational integrity," "doing the right things the first time," "serving others," and "being effective risk-takers." This executive then utilized these key phrases in as many meetings as possible and in private one-on-one meetings with other executives. The purpose of this list is to make new executives better understand what is expected of them and what will be the key themes and values of the changes that they will initiate. Having five to eight ideas for changes that can be readily accomplished provides a logical and effective means of gaining a foothold in the bureaucracy and developing a reputation as an executive of action.
- After the third month (3), new executives should write a summation of key organizational problems or issues and present it to the management of the organization, or to the divisional management team. The third month is the optimum time for a summation because if it were done earlier, it would lack some of the more covert problems

and would read roughly the same as a list of problems identified during the interview process. Also, by the end of the third month, new executives should have had the opportunity to meet personally with all of the other key executives within the organization.

- After the seventh month (7), new executives should formally articulate a specific short-term plan of action she/he would take the organization through.

The time frames for the 1-1-3-7 guide may differ slightly for each new executive, but the concepts are the same. Key issues such as a union organizational drive, a budget cycle, or impending employee reductions may speed the timetable up substantially. The quality of the previous executive's management of and departure from the post may also affect the time frame. However, and whenever, the 1-1-3-7 guide is executed, new executives must have a plan of action with specific deadlines and parameters.

Display strengths. Show everyone why they hired you. If financial management is your forte, then get involved in financial feasibility studies. If you excel at developing interpersonal relationships, start getting to know your staff and other employees. If working with physicians is your expertise, then focus on the medical staff. The idea behind displaying your strength is simply building a reputation of competence, knowledge, and experience.

Be cautious. Negative personality traits such as impatience and stubbornness are inexcusable during the honeymoon period. Be aware that everyone is watching and listening so you must apply the best techniques imaginable to win everyone's approval.

Build interpersonal influence. New executives should observe the qualities in leaders, both formal and informal, of the organization who give them interpersonal influence and then ascertain who these leaders are. Then, they should enlist these leaders to become a nucleus of support for the new policies, practices, and directions that they plan to implement. One new CEO assembled a list of influential leaders by simply asking the opinions of subordinate managers. This list gave the executive a good sense of what the organization valued in interpersonal leadership style and to whom the executive could turn for help.

Assemble your new team quickly. New executives should assess the existing managers quickly, decide who stays and who goes, hire replacements if needed, and state their expectations for the team's performance. Within the context of these decisions, executives must consider the complexity of the organization and weigh the risks of keeping some staff members against the dangers of not having access to the valuable information the dismissed staff members have. One CEO took so much time assembling a new team that he left for another position 15 months after he recruited the last executive. There was not enough time for him to implement his values and affect the culture of the organization. As a result, the CEO who followed him found the organization's management unwilling to take any risks or become excited with any of her initiatives.

Aside from the general difficulties of starting a new post, employees of the organization who have been promoted to executive positions face an even greater challenge. The newly promoted executive may be encumbered with excess baggage from past decisions and may have rivals or enemies looking for ways to undermine her/him, which could make assuming the authority of their new role difficult. Promoted executives should develop managerial themes that:

- build on past successes and target specific areas including improving quality of services, increasing cost effectiveness, changing the organizational structure, or enhancing relations with the medical staff;

- emphasize their intimate knowledge of the organization and their ability to move the organization ahead without losing momentum. Of course, if the institution is in such a state of disarray that total turnaround is needed, then themes that emphasize stability and continuity will not work. Instead, the newly promoted executive will need to introduce themes of change and renewal; and
- exercise extreme caution if others approach them about past promises and deals made by the previous executive. This initial period is not the time to feel forced into actions that may not be beneficial. Ideally, these issues can be cleared up in the interview process by clarifying with the hiring authority so that the newly hired executive may begin with a clean slate.

Chapter Fourteen

THE OFFICE

Remember that your behavior, whatever type of entertainment setting is chosen—breakfast, lunch, dinner, party, holiday bash—is always under scrutiny. Good manners and etiquette apply especially in these seemingly unofficial settings. Ironically, it may be even more important to scrutinize your every word, as well as what you wear and how much you drink or eat, in these pseudosocial situations, where you might be tempted to let down your guard, than even in the obviously business face-to-face meeting with your boss in his office.

Jan Yager in *Business Protocol: How to
Survive and Succeed in Business* (1991)

E XECUTIVES SPEND TWO-THIRDS of their waking time during the workweek in the office. For many executives, the office has become witness to their career highs and lows and has provided the space in which they can develop or hone their managerial identity and skills. For the rank and file, the executive office is the "ivory tower" or the enigma that inspires curiosity and envy, especially among staff members who have never been in it or have no reason to penetrate it.

Over the years, the office has become an extension of the executive's personality, style, and even home. In fact, some executives work so much that they have converted their offices to give them a home-like environment in which they can relax, reenergize, and escape. However, a home-like office could be counterproductive because it promotes comfort too much that it lulls its occupant instead of stimulating her/him. Too much comfort often translates to complacency and carelessness.

The concepts in this chapter debunk comfortability—with the home-like office, position, status, or power—and extol attentiveness to careful work, behavior, speech, and social and professional interaction in the office.

GENERAL OFFICE PROTOCOLS

Be cautious with humor. An office is a place for work, not a club for trying out new comedy material, so executives must use careful judgement when wanting to deliver humorous anecdotes or jokes. While having a sense of humor is healthy and often necessary, it can have negative effects when unchecked. Jokes that demean and disrespect ethnicities, gender, religious and political affiliations, and handicap or have sexual connotations should never be shared in the office, or in any professional setting, because they would only offend, alienate, and make uncomfortable peers and employees. Furthermore, they do not add to productivity, increase morale, or improve relationships.

Never borrow money from coworkers. Loans between coworkers are dangerous because they put the lender and the borrower in uncomfortable positions. Although borrowing is a sign that staff members are at ease enough with each other to engage in such a personal transaction, it is also a sign of future unrest among them.

Decorate the office appropriately. Although customizing the office to reflect the executive's personal style and preference is permissible, doing so should not conflict with the general decor of the organization. For example, displaying several trophies, awards, and family photographs is fine, but mounting multiple paraphernalia along the walls is excessive and distracting. One CEO, after moving from a rural location to an urban medical center, heavily decorated his office with multiple mounted fish and various photographs of hunting and fishing trips. While appropriate in his former hospital, this display looked very out of place in the city. Another example is when a public relations executive filled shelves in her offices with stuffed animals. While this decor was suitable in her former office in a children's hospital, the display looked inappropriate in her new organization that did not even have a pediatric department.

Determine the appropriateness of office traditions. Departments, teams, and office suites develop their own practices to show and strengthen their work dynamic and personal camaraderie. Executives must take part in these practices, or at least respect them if she/he are exempt from such activities.

A new chief executive who joins an office that has a well-established and much-loved tradition should first survey the practices and determine if they are appropriate for the office setting. Although these morale-boosting activities are fun and fundamental, they do not sometimes subscribe to the rules and mindset of the organization. If the executive finds the practice inappropriate, she/he must be careful about eliminating it or exacting unreasonable changes. For example, when a CEO arrived at his new hospital, he found that the support staff and the executives in the office suite had a monthly potluck lunch. Although the CEO found the lunches enjoyable and participated during his first two months, he later stopped them after he determined that these lunches sent the wrong message to the rest of the hospital: The office suite staff is unprofessional, lax, and too festive for the work setting. Food odors permeating the executive suite and wafting into the surrounding areas were uncontrollable and the support staff could not do their work during the morning because they were all busy preparing the food. In addition, some visitors to the suite implied to the CEO that these lunches were unprofessional. Before he ended the tradition, the CEO first gave his staff a detailed explanation of his reasons and offered an alternative activity, which was well received by staff and is still being practiced now.

Ensure the physical appropriateness of the office. Consider the following.

- Support staff members are eating at their desks and the odors of the food are permeating the entire area.
- The coffee room is littered by dirty dishes, liquid spills, and strewn towels.
- The office areas are cluttered with reading material and opened boxes and the garbage receptacles are overflowing.

Although the above scenarios seem minor and are more a nuisance rather than an organizational threat, they can spark discomfort among office occupants. Although all office occupants must take part in cleaning up after themselves and minimizing the clutter, executives are responsible for providing a well-ventilated lunch area to contain food odor.

Maintain professionalism. Executives must realize that their power is very intimidating and must not be used, consciously and unconsciously, to their advantage. For example, support staff members who buy fundraising tickets or items from executives may do so only because they feel obligated. Similarly, executives must not ask support staff to do them personal favors.

Among executives, too much casualness in speech and behavior should not be the norm.

Receive guests appropriately. The neatness of the office; the respect, hospitality, and courtesy shown by staff, the executive's punctuality, even the standard amenities—coffee or tea—offered are all factors in making the guest feels welcomed in the office suite. The quality of the guest reception usually reflects the quality of the executive's administration.

PROTOCOLS FOR MAINTAINING PROFESSIONAL RELATIONSHIPS

With Peer Executives

- In most organizations, chief executives work together closely not only figuratively but literally as they are all confined in one space—the executive suite. Because they spend so much time together, some of these executives form friendships that go on outside of the office and sometimes involve their families—they socialize and play together. Although these friendships are a strong cog in the machinery of team building, they can also be harmful because executives can become too comfortable with one another and develop an excessive degree of informality that is carried back to the workplace. This relaxed atmosphere can be counterproductive and disruptive, especially when the team has to deal with difficult issues.
- Executives may form cliques. These cliques will often plan their strategies in social settings and seem conspiratorial back in the workplace.
- Spouses may form such close friendships that they may share information heard in confidence, which could be damaging to other executives in the team.

135

The chief executive should carefully consider how off-hours socializing opportunities are designed for the executive team. Although spending time out of the office to get to know one another seems social, these events are still considered a business function in the context of team building, and because they are work related, all executives should act professionally and cautiously. Chief executives must be cautious not to create the perception that some team members have more access to them than others do. If this apparent access seems to be the result of outside opportunities to socialize, it can be most destructive to office morale. An imperfect line often must be drawn between chief executives and their subordinate executives; particularly when it comes to friendships. Chief executives must remember that they have ultimate authority in their organizations. In reality, friendships that are not based on the equal footing of both parties cannot be easily maintained. It is, indeed, lonely at the top. Friendships, although possible between people at different levels within the workplace, are very difficult to maintain once someone reaches the top.

With Support Staff

Many of the protocols below are predicated on the assumption that executives are employees not owners of organizations. A slightly different set of protocols may apply if the administrative assistant works for an executive-owner. The relationship between the executive and the administrative assistant is strictly professional. Therefore, administrative assistants should never be expected or asked to perform duties outside of her/his professional duties.

Although administrative assistants are very important to executives, many executives treat their assistants as "office equipment" or as an executive perq. Although many executives claim to value their assistants, few executives act as if they do and some even equate the degree of respect they give with the assistant's level of usefulness. The following protocols spell out the proper way administrative assistants must be treated.

Share information. Executives should inform assistants the rationale and background of issues or decisions and discuss with them the direction the organization is headed. Doing so not only shows your effort to educate the assistants but makes good business sense: Informed assistants are better assistants, especially in your absence, and can provide additional support for your policies.

Don't treat them as servants. Balancing the executives' personal checkbook, buying and wrapping gifts for her/his spouse, placing or taking personal telephone calls, picking up laundry or handling chores for family members are not appropriate administrative assistant functions. Some exceptions to this no-personal-errand rule apply, however. For example, when an executive returns late from a meeting, is due to go to another meeting, and needs to drop off her automobile in front of the building, she may appropriately ask the assistant to park it. Similarly, ordering and delivering lunch when executives need to work through the lunch period is an appropriate request, and so is preparing and serving coffee or tea for a meeting. A general rule is that administrative assistants can be asked to get coffee or lunch or to help in other ways as a favor to the executive, not as a condition of employment. The executive should return the favor when the assistant is likewise occupied.

Show common courtesy. Executives tend to be informal and relaxed with their assistants, especially when they have been working with each other a long time. Even routine interpersonal exchanges, however, should be courteous to show the assistant is not being taken for granted.

Keep away from personal issues. Executives should keep discussions of personal affairs out of the office. Although light-hearted exchanges about family or personal interests are a good way to get to know each other, more serious and intimate issues, such as marital and financial problems, should be avoided. Changing the subject is a safe way to extricate yourself from such a discussion.

Manage perceptions. Executives should make every effort to avoid situations, such as going out to lunch and working on the weekends with the assistant frequently, that could potentially be misconstrued as a personal relationship. This perception is especially real when the assistant is of the opposite sex. Touching is also a frequently misinterpreted gesture. Patting on the back or casual draping of the arm on the shoulders may seem innocent and may be well intentioned to the people engaged in them, but to onlookers they can mean something else, so remember that any physical contact is risky.

Clarify expectations. Because, in essence, the executive and the assistant are a team, they must understand and discuss each other's expectations including the necessity of working though lunch, staying late, or working over a weekend, and the importance of confidentiality.

Do not give intimate gifts. Lingerie, perfume, gloves, scarves, and expensive jewelry are not appropriate gifts. Although the inappropriateness of these gifts seems obvious, some executives have fallen victims to them. For example, a vice president in a Midwestern hospital presented his assistant with a camisole at the office Christmas party.

Appropriate gifts are reasonable in price and intent such as food items, books, desk items, or gift certificates. An expensive gift might send the unintended message that the cost of the gift is a measure of the executive's personal appreciation. Also, expensive gifts may make the administrative assistant feel obligated to try to match the expense of the gift.

PROTOCOLS FOR BUSINESS-RELATED SOCIAL OCCASION

Part of being an executive is being social because it is one of the most effective ways she/he can get to know a peer, or an employee; make business connections; or garner support. Receptions, lunches, and dinners thrown by a multitude of hosts and for a multitude of reasons are a regular reality for the executive and, at times, her/his spouse. Representing the organization well is a definite mandate for the executive and her/his companion. The protocols below are some guidelines on how to mix socially.

Do not overindulge. Executives should not attend cocktail parties or receptions for the purpose of eating and drinking. After all, all business-related social events are pure business. A safe rule is to partake in one alcoholic drink and indulge in other nonalcoholic beverages. Consider eating something light beforehand to take the edge off hunger so you can enjoy the carefully prepared food leisurely. Grazing continuously at the food table is uncouth and ill mannered.

Mingle. Mingling is a skill that can be learned and *must* be learned if you are an executive, even if you are not outgoing by nature. Introducing yourself to various people and making small talks thereafter are imperative to making a business connection in these social events. Small talk topics include sports, travel, or current affairs. Avoid discussing religion, politics, and social controversies. Three basic concepts of mingling are:

1. circling or "working" the room;
2. engaging someone in small talk; and
3. disengaging without seeming rude.

Pay attention to details. Executives can improve the impression they give by following a few simple guidelines below.

- Hold drinks in the left hand so the right hand is dry and free to shake hands.
- Introduce the older person first. If you are unsure of the ages, make a quick guess.
- If you are hosting the event, arrive early, stay late, and mingle with everyone at the party, even with people you do not know. If necessary, skip the dessert so you can have time to greet everyone.

Be gracious. Executives who are hosting a business lunch should try to make arrangements in advance, including making sure the server knows who should receive the check. Restaurants with which the executive is familiar are a safe choice. The host should arrive early and should escort the guests to the table, instead of waiting at the table.

Avoid drinking at lunch. Although offering the guest the opportunity to order an alcoholic drink is common courtesy, the host should carefully consider the potential negative ramifications of having even one drink at lunch. The host should also indicate first if she/he plans to have an alcoholic drink. A good rule is to never have any kind of alcoholic beverage if one plans to return to the office to avoid the perception that she/he has "boozed it up" during lunch. One CEO always told the executive team that they should feel free to have a drink at lunch, but they should then take the rest of the day off and work at home.

Observe proper decorum at the table. During a business lunch, executives should avoid disputes with restaurant staff. The lunch should be a sidelight to the business agenda.

Respect others' time. Early in the lunch, the host should try to find out any time constraints the other parties may have. If time is a factor, move into the business agenda shortly after the drinks have arrived. Postponing business discussions until late in the meal is inconsiderate because some people may not be able to stay that long.

Do not argue over the check. Although the ethical purist may wish to avoid all business lunches so as not to have to grapple with this problem, most executives will encounter such occasions. A generally accepted rule is to allow a salesperson, consultant, vendor, or the person for whom the lunch was beneficial to pick up the check. Do not debate over the tip either. If the occasion is a mutual get together, then split the check and tip evenly.

Do not smoke. Many restaurants today are now smoke free, which eliminates (1) the need for smokers to ask permission from their companion and (2) the awkwardness nonsmokers feel when disapproving.

Chapter Fifteen

CULTURAL AND GENDER DIVERSITY

This focus on changing diverse people has created difficulties for many people of color, women, differently abled, gay,
and ethnically diverse people who want to maintain their own
cultural heritages as they move ahead in their careers. For
while such individuals can often maintain their diverse identi-
ties at the entry level, the range of acceptable behavior narrows as one moves up the career ladder.

Marilyn Loden and Judy B. Rosener in
*Workforce America: Managing Employee
Diversity as a Vital Resource* (1991)

IN 1987, THE HUDSON Institute published a landmark
study titled *Workforce 2000: Work and Workers for the 21st
Century.* The study noted three factors that would change
the face of the healthcare workforce in the new century:

1. "non-whites will make up 29 percent ... [which
   is] ... twice their current share";
2. "immigrants will represent the largest share of the
   increase ... since the first World War"; and
3. women will make up 47 percent.

Now, thirteen years later, the predictions set forth in *Workforce 2000* have become realities. The U.S. Department of Labor's report, *Futurework*, with data taken from the U.S. Census Bureau, states that:

- The fastest growing minority group is Latinos.
- 820,000 immigrants are projected to arrive in the United States annually, and two out of three of them will join the workforce immediately.
- Women's participation in the workforce has been steadily increasing, while men's participation has decreased.

In 1992, the American College of Healthcare Executives and National Association of Health Services Executives conducted a study titled *A Race/Ethnic Comparison of Career Attainment in Healthcare Management*. In 1997, with collaboration from the Association of Hispanic Healthcare Executives and Institute for Diversity in Health Management, the study was revisited, which yielded information about the changing faces and gender of healthcare leadership. The top positions—CEO, COO/senior vice president—are held by:

- 23 percent of African-American and Latino women;
- 35 percent of Caucasian women; and
- 15 percent of Asian women.

The statistics listed above solidify the theory I posed in the first edition of this book: The healthcare industry is only going to become increasingly diverse. Therefore, its leaders must prepare itself to manage and meet the needs and challenges of diversity, and must realize that diversity is beneficial and necessary in all levels of the organization.

Although the term diversity often connotes merely the variations of racial and cultural backgrounds, its true definition is more extensive in that it refers to differences in age, physical and mental abilities, gender, sexual orientation, and religious and political affiliation. The protocols submitted in this chapter are universal and timeless in that they are applicable to all types of diversity issues whether a leader encounters them in the beginning of 2000 or halfway through this century.

The foundation of all the protocols in this chapter is respect. Respect is both a product and a producer of curiosity about people who come from a different culture; who practice a different tradition; who subscribe to a different set of beliefs; or who, simply, vary physically. Respect cannot be faked or given facetiously, which is a view contrary to what a well-known search consultant once suggested to healthcare workers who directly provide patient care. The consultant suggested that workers only have to *act* as if they are happy to help; they do not have to actually *feel* happy. Unfortunately, a variation of this theory manifests itself in some executive's approach to diversity in the workplace: "I don't like or agree with diversity, but I have to pretend to like it to get what I want." Although this approach is workable in the short term, it is a major catalyst for unrest within the organization because pretenses can be easily uncovered and they are the weakest foundation for developing long-term relationships. Respect, rather than a more generic like, is necessary because it encourages treatment of people as individuals and discourages easy belief in stereotypes. Variation is not tantamount to inferiority.

PROTOCOLS FOR CULTURAL DIVERSITY

Although the explosion of multiculturalism has inspired sensitivity and receptiveness rhetoric, demanded mediation and compromise, and created equal employment opportunity laws, more national initiatives still need to be designed. But further advancement must first occur locally, even in small doses.

Promote diversity. All executives should talk about diversity within their own teams to acclimate them about its necessity, importance, and contribution. Human resources executives could become active advocates by (1) keeping the team aware of diversity issues faced by the work force and by (2) speaking up in support of programs, in or out of the organization, that promote advancement of minority employees through hiring, training, and educating.

Discuss diversity. One of the main reasons that racial tension, or any other socio-political issues, between or among any groups remains an uncomfortable topic in organization is that it is not discussed and, hence, not properly dealt with and resolved. According to George Davis and Gregg Watson in *Black Life in Corporate America,* "On the surface blacks and whites get along quite well in most corporate settings .... They laugh together and call each other 'friend.' However, blacks are often oppressed by this silence on race. Their careers and morale are affected by this thing that they cannot mention."

Although prejudice—racial, gender, cultural, etc.—is personal, it is also divisive because it is based on pure perception and fear. A candid dialogue, especially when there are no conflicts, and an ongoing education or training on diversity issues bring out hidden issues and encourage true, even if slow, acceptance rather than quiet tolerance.

Stay informed. National and local news or magazines are some of the more accessible resources of current issues and trends faced by minority groups in the United States. Being aware of these issues prepares you for their ramifications on your staff specifically and your organization as a whole.

Practice affirmative action. Minorities—including women and the physically disabled—must be hired or promoted to management-level positions. An organization that practices affirmative action hiring shows that it is truly committed to diversity because it stays attuned with the needs of its work force and gives minorities an opportunity to share in the successes of the organization. A manager, or executive, from a minority background is beneficial because many healthcare organizations serve minority populations and communities. Therefore, the manager is likely to have insight or resources that the organization can tap into. Organizations that have worked aggressively to employ people with physical disabilities also report remarkable positive returns. Even before the passage of the Americans with Disabilities Act (ADA) in 1992, numerous healthcare employers were successfully employing people with physical disabilities in various positions.

Hiring the most qualified candidate is a reasonable business practice. Executives, however, should consider which qualifications are required and which are preferred, or can be learned, because rigid expectations more likely disqualify candidates who may lack a minor criterion but are otherwise ideal for the position. For reasons too involved and too numerous to list, many minorities did not, and do not, have the opportunities to acquire the education, skills, and experience required to compete on the same level as others who have had the privilege. This deficiency does not make minorities incompetent, but it does work against their favor. Affirmative action hiring bridges this gap.

This hiring practice, however, is controversial and often raises protests because some executives equate affirmative action to an organization's obligation to meet a quota of minority employees, regardless of competency or qualification. To many minorities, on the other hand, affirmative action provides an opportunity to advance, monetarily and career wise, in the work force and status in life; an opportunity which they are often denied whether or not they are qualified. Some minorities believe that "qualifications" is a code word that executives, who are mostly Caucasian males, use as an excuse to avoid hiring them. Although in some instances this generalization about the term is true, some instances also disprove this belief; therefore executives must manage this general perception by keeping an open mind and altering their hiring practices.

Executives must often take some calculated risks to introduce diversity into their organizations. For executives who are risk averse, they can reduce the risk of employing unknowns by providing the existent staff with in-house, skill-development training and partnering with community programs that can provide volunteers and interns.

Celebrate other cultures. An organization-wide celebration of diversity is one of the best illustrations of acceptance. "Theme Days," in which a specific culture—ethnic or not—is exhibited through food, art, music, and literature are one of the most popular ways of educating people about a different origin and practice. These theme days are often held in cafeterias and often receive favorable responses from employees, patients, visitors, and executives. Special holidays and month-long observances must be commemorated or recognized including Dr. Martin Luther King's birthday, Cinco de Mayo, Chinese New Year, Ramadan, National American Indian Heritage Month, Asian Pacific History Month, International Woman's Day, National Women's History Month, Black History Month, National Hispanic Heritage Month, National Disability Employment Awareness Month, etc.

A cultural diversity day is another type of celebration but, unlike theme days, does not focus on any particular culture. The idea behind the day is to recognize the collective diversity of the organization. One hospital posted a list of names of employees who were willing to talk about their backgrounds. A number of these employees shared stories about themselves and/or their relatives and their experiences in the United States.

Develop and support diversity management programs. The organization's Human Resources department must establish a conflict management program that addresses and resolves diversity grievances; a training program that enhances understanding of and sensitivity to diversity issues; and anti-harassment programs that discourages anyone from telling culturally insensitive jokes, teasing, or stereotyping. Members of various minority groups should participate in the development and presentation of these programs. Executives should support them by attending and encouraging employees to respect them.

Assemble a diverse board. The board should mirror the community it serves so executives must recruit members from backgrounds similar to the organization's service population to ensure fair representation of views and decisions.

Improve the physical design of the facility. Signage inside and outside the organization must be understandable to non-English speakers either through multilingual translations or graphic representation. For example, an organization that serves a predominantly Spanish-speaking population must make sure that signs also can be read in Spanish (for those who do not communicate in English), and pictures or symbols of rules such as No Exit, No Smoking, or Do Not Use Elevator must be easily seen to ensure safety. Wheelchair accessible entrances, exits, and hallways; doors that automatically open with a push of a button; Braille elevator buttons; telecommunications device for the hearing impaired (TTY and TDD) make the organization sensitive to the needs of its employees, patients, visitors, and executives.

Participate in community programs that enhance diversity. Consider an adopt-a-school program in which the organization uses its resources and staff volunteers to provide training, workshops, or mentoring at area public schools with a lot of minority students. Executives should also encourage, recruit, and welcome minority volunteers. The presence of minority volunteers sends a positive message to the community and makes patients and visitors, especially people from minority backgrounds, feel more comfortable. In addition, executives should offer financial and staff support to social and sports activities that involve diverse groups because company-sponsored events or teams are often an excellent mechanism to assemble a diverse team and enhance organizational teamwork.

PROTOCOLS FOR GENDER DIVERSITY

Sexual harassment, pay inequities, the glass ceiling, the boy's club, and the mommy track are terms that continue to be part of the everyday language of the workplace. Although women have made contributions that have greatly improved the quality of life all over the world, much of the world continue to be patriarchal and its social conditions still do not give women the same opportunities afforded to their male counterparts. In the United States alone, six in ten women are in the work force, but the majority of CEOs are men.

A new trend in the workforce is rising, however, as Audrey Edwards summarized: "It is clearly no longer a man's world, and certainly not a white man's world, given that [the white man] is expected to account for only 32 percent of the entering work force by 2000." More stay-at-home mothers or wives are resuming their careers or starting their own business at home. More early- and mid-careerists are going back to school to enhance their skills or jumpstart another career. More women are heading traditionally male-dominated industries such as car dealership, construction, and even healthcare. The protocols below promote harmony between the genders.

Avoid stereotypes. Executives, male and female, should beware of and should discourage gender biases at all times. For example, when electing a project manager for the organization's child-care center, a female manager should not be elected because of societal expectations that a woman is "more caring"; rather, the decision should be based on competence. Similarly, subconscious adherence to gender duties, such as women cook and clean while men lift and move heavy objects, is old fashioned and must be avoided. For a male executive to expect his female administrative assistant to make and bring him coffee on a daily basis is sexist and unnecessary.

Be mindful of office decor. Minimizing illustration of gender types in the office minimizes the focus on gender differences. Decorations, although such a mundane element, set the attitude of any workplace. Posters, photographs, art, or desk accessories must not be marked with pithy sayings that are derogatory to the opposite gender (e.g., "It takes two men to do a woman's job.") or subscribe to stereotypes (e.g., "I earn it and my wife spends it."). Although these supposedly "humorous" remarks can be empowering or may not be mean spirited, they can also be offensive and can encourage retaliatory attitude.

Abstain from chivalry. Common courtesy such as holding the door for followers when you reach it first or volunteering to press the elevator button when the other person is unable to reach it is socially acceptable. However, chivalrous tendencies, especially of men, such as pulling out chairs for female colleagues or offering to carry heavy objects are fodder for misinterpretation. Similarly, handshaking should be equal in that men and women should not wait for the other to initiate a handshake. A firm handshake is always in order; it should not be softened or hardened to accommodate the gender or perceived strength of the receiver.

Eschew behavioral archetypes. Societal mindset labels men's determination as *assertiveness*, while it calls the same drive in women *aggressiveness*. Of course, the connotation for assertiveness is almost always positive, while aggressiveness is almost always negative. This unfair labeling is a result of the way we as a society have been conditioned to accept gender types. According to these types, women are supposed to be meek, while men are

151

supposed to be obstinate. Therefore, anyone who does not fit into the category is subject to negative labeling or called as an aberration. As an executive, your responsibility is to follow your own archetypes based on work performance and ability, not societal biases.

Discourage sexist language. Affectionate terms or titles, slang, vernacular phrases, popular terms may all be considered sexist language. Language continues to evolve and so are the faces and gender of the work place; therefore, terms that were commonly used and employee approved in the last decades may not be received so innocently anymore. Every word and phrase have connotations, so choose yours carefully.

Beware of gender-based professional groups. Gender-specific professional groups empower men and women to advance in their careers—by providing outlets for skill training, building networks, and finding mentors—and teach them skills to balance their home, work, and social responsibilities. Although these groups are generally advantageous, a caveat is in order. Too much involvement in these groups can interfere with work responsibilities and its gender-specific emphasis could promote gender schisms.

PROTOCOLS FOR A SEXUAL-HARASSMENT FREE WORKPLACE

The nature of the healthcare industry creates two challenges that are unusual to other industries. First, physicians provide services in organizations that may not be their employers. Although many physicians are female, most are still male whose support staff and nurses are mostly female. As a result, the risk of sexual harassment and prevalence of sexist attitudes are greater within this group, and the organization cannot exact the same anti-gender bias rules on the physicians as it does on its employees. Second, the executive team in healthcare organizations almost always consists of at least one female—the vice president of Nursing. In other industries, the senior management almost always comprises male members. These deviations prime healthcare organizations for much trickier sexual harassment conditions. Consider the following examples.

- Example A: A male CFO found nude drawings of women on the Internet. The CFO disregarded the fact that several members of the team are women, and printed out the drawings and brought them to the meeting to show the men on the team. Many of the men and all the women were appalled. The CEO severely reprimanded the CFO and ordered him to make a public apology. The CFO lost the credibility, influence, and respect he had established within the organization.
- Example B: A male doctor worked in an office with a female assistant. He often complimented her on her choice of clothing or accessory and told her she looked great. Although none of his remarks were sexually suggestive or were meant to be other than complimentary, the assistant increasingly became very uncomfortable around him. Although she finally expressed her discomfort and he agreed to cease the comments immediately, their relationship never returned to the friendly rapport they once had. Eventually, the doctor left the office.

Sexual harassment refers to all forms of conduct, including verbal and nonverbal acts, that threaten, make uncomfortable, or demean people of both genders. Because some men interpret sexual harassment differently—harassment is aggressive and hostile and meant to injure—they do not equate sexual innuendo or teasing to sexual harassment; hence, they vigorously deny the charge. The law states that sexual harassment condition occurs in the workplace even when no direct harassment occurs between two employees; a sexually charged atmosphere that makes any employee uncomfortable is basis enough.

Follow a strict hands-off rule. Any touch other than a handshake can be misinterpreted. Embracing; resting arms on shoulders; rubbing backs, arms, shoulders, or hair; holding hands; and tickling are all improper and unprofessional. If the touching is consensual, it could make witnesses uncomfortable. If the receiver is a subordinate, she/he may be too intimidated to tell the giver to stop. Either scenario proves that touching has no place in any settings in or out of the office sanctioned by the organization.

Avoid exchanges with sexual connotations. Looks, stares, glimpses, and body language that suggest attraction; discussions that refer to or involve sex; jokes that have sexual meanings; and distribution of sexually explicit material through photocopies or e-mail must all be avoided to decrease the risk of harassment charges.

Practice romantic abstinence. For many adults, the workplace is the easiest and most comfortable place in which to meet a multitude of diverse and interesting people. It is where people form life-long friendships, business partnerships, and possibly romantic relationships. However, in the interest of managing perception and remaining fair, executives should not partake in the chances of forming romantic relationships in the workplace. Why is romantic abstinence necessary? Consider the following reasons.

- When one, or both, partner holds a management position, the relationship invites all sorts of negative accusations including favoritism, unfair distribution of resources, trading of corporate secrets, conspiracy, and bias. All the negativity would directly affect productivity.
- Personal or professional disputes, such as unequal pay, responsibility, and recognition, between the couple may

surface in decision-making processes and negatively affect them.

- Employees may find being direct and candid to one partner about the other very difficult, even when necessary.
- When a partner is performing poorly and the other is excelling, the leadership team is faced with the dilemma of what to do with the poor performer.
- The couple can become too informal with each other in the workplace.
- The couple's productivity may decline as they become preoccupied with each other.

Abide by the law. Federal law mandates all organizations to establish a written sexual harassment policy. The policy must stress the organization's anti-harassment stance and must detail its procedures for investigating, determining, and responding to charges. Within the limits of the policy, executives must mete out appropriate disciplinary action.

As mentioned before, managing others' perception is the surest way to vanish gossip, minimize suspicion, and, most importantly, abort charges of sexual harassment. When traveling on business with the opposite sex, executives sometimes may have to add another person. If this arrangement is not possible, however, they should at least make sure that the same person is not a constant business companion. When working late or on the weekends with the opposite sex, the executive must make sure to leave earlier or later than the other person.

REFERENCES

1. American College of Healthcare Executives and National Association of Health Services Executives. 1997. A *Race/Ethnic Comparison of Career Attainment in Healthcare Management.* Chicago: ACHE.

2. Davis, G., and G. Watson. 1985. *Black Life in Corporate America: Swimming in the Mainstream.* New York: Anchor Books/Doubleday.

3. Edwards, A. 1991. *Working Woman.*

4. Hudson Institute. 1987. *Workforce 2000: Work and Workers for the 21st Century.* Indianapolis, IN: Hudson Institute.

5. Jones, Laurie. 1999. "Women in Healthcare: Promotions on the Rise." *www.womenconnect.com.*

6. Loden, M., and J. B. Rosener. 1991. *Workforce America: Managing Employee Diversity as a Vital Resource.* Homewood, IL: Business One Irwin.

7. U.S. Department of Labor. 1999. *Futurework: Trends and Challenges for Work in the 21st Century.* [www.dol.gov/dol/asp/public/futurework/report; visited 4/24/00).

8. "Women Heading More Companies." 1998. *www.Nando.com/newsroom.*

EPILOGUE

Negative energy is a depleter, causing hopelessness, help-lessness, and powerlessness. With negative energy, people see no possibilities or choices; they are resistant to change and use their energy against the manager and the organization. Negative energy is soon exhausted, leaving little or no energy at all.

Arthur C. Beck and Ellis D. Hillmar in
Positive Management Practices (1986)

A PERSON WHO THOROUGHLY understands her/his thought processes, ideals, rationale for behavior, and tendencies for action is already a subscriber to the protocols submitted in this book. Therefore, the underlying message of attaining executive excellence is simple: Get to know yourself well so you can get to know others and serve them better. Of course, a complete picture of yourself is easier said than seen, so you need tools that would guide your search.

Figure EI: Johari Window

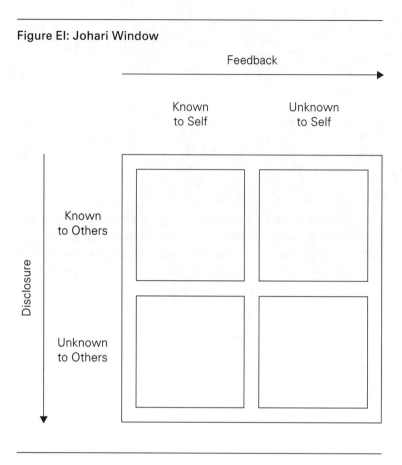

SELF-IMPROVEMENT   TOOLS

Tool 1: The Johari Window

The Johari Window, named after its creators Joseph Luft and Harrington Ingham, is designed to reveal certain truths about a person through interaction with and self-disclosure to someone else. The window is divided into four window panes, which stand for a person's self-awareness: (1) open, (2) hidden, (3) blind, and (4) unknown (see Figure EI). The "open" pane represents things that are known to everyone including the person. The "hidden" pane represents things that are known only by the person, but are either falsified or untold. The "blind" pane represents things known to everyone but the person (a blind spot). The "unknown" pane represents things unknown to everyone. The lines that divide the panes can be adjusted to either widen or narrow each pane as more disclosure occurs. For example, if an executive discloses to someone else that she/he does not like organization-sponsored luncheons, then the open quadrant widens and the hidden quadrant narrows. Similarly, if a person reveals to the executive that the executive's assertiveness intimidates everyone else, then the executive's blind quadrant narrows and the open quadrant widens. The object of the Johari Window is to get to know yourself by interacting and communicating with people around you. Use the window provided here or construct your own, then recruit a partner who is willing to give you insight into your personality as an executive.

Tool 2: The Mentor

A mentor is not only a mirror of your professional aspirations but also an evaluator of your professional shortcomings. Choosing a mentor must be done carefully because the advice and criticism of your mentor are crucial in your progress as a leader. Ideally, a mentor should be someone trustworthy, experienced, and who invites challenges. Consider becoming a mentor yourself. The experience would not only enrich someone else's career, but would give you an opportunity to assess your own mistakes.

Tool 3: Continuing Education

Seek out and participate in programs, seminars, and workshops that either sharpen or add to your skill set and knowledge. Read healthcare management-related literature constantly to keep up with trends that affect your organization, market, and career.

Expertise is not a license to stop learning; in fact, it is a product of a life-long curiosity. Continuing education enhances the executive's chances of job retention and consistent promotion.

Tool 4: Self-Management

The world, our lives, and the way we see both elements are constantly changing. Our multiple roles as a spouse, a parent, a child, a sibling, a leader, a neighbor, and a friend dictate our views, expectations, and responses. Self-management is the idea behind taking charge of ourselves when our roles conflict with our expectations. It can also be defined as our emotional intelligence. This method may be one of the most difficult for busy leaders because it requires attention and focus. Many executives have developed styles and approaches that have become deeply ingrained. Changing these behaviors takes enormous effort and single mindedness.

Tool 5: Networks

Executives should take every opportunity to network with other industry professionals. A network of professionals can provide much-needed feedback, background information, expertise, and/ or volunteer to test new processes. In addition, in close-knit networks, professionals openly share and discuss their successes and failures from which executives can learn.

Tool 6: 360-Degree Evaluations and Psychological Assessments

The 360-degree evaluation, in which one receives behavioral feedback from peers and coworkers who are above and below one's position, is an appraisal of strengths and weaknesses. This method of evaluation is more comprehensive than a traditional evaluation done only by a superior.

Psychological assessments and style inventories such as the Myers-Briggs Type Indicator and the various Hogan Assessments Systems also provide valuable insight into a person's styles and behavioral characteristics.

Executive excellence is always buoyed by a certain amount of luck. Meeting the right people, being someplace at opportune moments, or discovering prospects are instances of pure luck rather than results of hard work and dedication. Unfortunately, luck is not a controllable element; hence, it is never consistent. Therefore, an executive has to rely more on skills to move forward. But are skills and a sprinkle of luck enough to excel in a service industry? Definitely not. The protocols submitted in this book act as the bridge to executive excellence. Although they are not absolute rules and must not be considered as a panacea, they are good prescriptions. The key to making these protocols work, however, is by receiving them with an open mind.

Appendix A

HUMAN RESOURCES
ETHICS QUESTIONNAIRE

The scenarios in this questionnaire reflect the same compromising, controversial, and complex human resources dilemmas in the workplace. These dilemmas examine:

- recruiting procedures that affect the final outcome of the employee search (see Questions 1, 3, and 4);
- "acceptable lying" in the office (see Questions 13, 19, 22, 23, and 24); and
- legal practices with ethical implications (see Questions 2, 5, 6, 8, 9, 10).

These questions demand thoughtful consideration because their implications are often great—they affect, and potentially change, lives of those involved. The executive's response to these scenarios often is the single greatest determining factor of her/his integrity in the eyes of colleagues, business partners, board members, superiors, and subordinates. Although organizational policies and human resources laws provide guidelines in responding to these scenarios, they are not often based on ethical standards or common human courtesy, which this book submits. Ultimately, the answers are dependent on the respondent's personal beliefs and value system. Therefore, no answer can be considered right or wrong.

Recommendation: This questionnaire gauges, not judges, the executive's human resources mindset. Its purpose is to fuel discussions and self-examinations, which would ultimately reveal an executive's decision-making paradigm and whether it fits legal and ethical standards of the organization or needs to be altered. The questionnaire could be completed three ways:

1. Individually. Executives sometimes realize their own strengths, weaknesses, and preferences only after encountering thought-provoking, self-assessment questions on paper. Alone, the executive can be uninhibited with her/his responses and would not need to worry about being scrutinized for "improper" office practices and judged for personal beliefs.
2. With a partner. Executives can choose a colleague who is willing to complete the questionnaire and discuss its results.
3. With a management team. Responses to the questions reveal each executive's ethical leanings and organization-wide discrepancies in the way departments are managed, policies are followed, and employees are treated.

1. Effective and efficient screening of applications and resumes matters. Your Employment Services division quickly reviews these applications and resumes and decides on which to keep and discard based on the initial review. Some of the applications and resumes are placed into a "dead" file, which means that the people to whom they belong will not be considered for any position. This is an acceptable practice.

Strongly Disagree	Disagree	Neither Disagree or Agree	Agree	Strongly Agree
1	2	3	4	5

2. Discussing family-related issues, such as relocation, with executive candidates is an acceptable practice.

Strongly Disagree	Disagree	Neither Disagree or Agree	Agree	Strongly Agree
1	2	3	4	5

3. Almost all external applicants deserve an explanation for their rejection when another applicant is selected.

Strongly Disagree	Disagree	Neither Disagree or Agree	Agree	Strongly Agree
1	2	3	4	5

4. Almost all internal applicants deserve an explanation for their rejection when another applicant is selected.

Strongly Disagree	Disagree	Neither Disagree or Agree	Agree	Strongly Agree
1	2	3	4	5

5. Designating certain positions to be filled by minority applicants is an acceptable practice.

Strongly Disagree	Disagree	Neither Disagree or Agree	Agree	Strongly Agree
1	2	3	4	5

6. Employees who are terminated during the probationary period of employment—for example, first three months—should have no rights to appeal or file a grievance according to organizational procedure.

Strongly Disagree	Disagree	Neither Disagree or Agree	Agree	Strongly Agree
1	2	3	4	5

7.   Certain applicants, such as convicted felons, should
     never be hired in positions that put them in direct
     contact with patients.

Strongly Disagree	Disagree	Neither Disagree or Agree	Agree	Strongly Agree
1	2	3	4	5

8.   Unless prohibited by written contract or statute,
     an employer should have the right to terminate an
     employee for any cause.

Strongly Disagree	Disagree	Neither Disagree or Agree	Agree	Strongly Agree
1	2	3	4	5

9.   Using hidden surveillance cameras to detect employee
     theft, especially when an incident of theft occurs, is an
     acceptable practice.

Strongly Disagree	Disagree	Neither Disagree or Agree	Agree	Strongly Agree
1	2	3	4	5

10. Random locker searches for illegal drugs is an acceptable practice as long as employees are informed beforehand of its possibility.

Strongly Disagree	Disagree	Neither Disagree or Agree	Agree	Strongly Agree
1	2	3	4	5

11. A competent human resources manager who becomes an active member of a politically extreme group, such as the Ku Klux Klan, should be terminated.

Strongly Disagree	Disagree	Neither Disagree or Agree	Agree	Strongly Agree
1	2	3	4	5

12. A competent night-shift boiler operator who becomes an active member of a politically extreme group, such as the Ku Klux Klan, should be terminated.

Strongly Disagree	Disagree	Neither Disagree or Agree	Agree	Strongly Agree
1	2	3	4	5

13. Making personal phone calls at work is an acceptable practice.

Strongly Disagree	Disagree	Neither Disagree or Agree	Agree	Strongly Agree
1	2	3	4	5

14. After employees reach ten or more years of service, an employer has a social responsibility to sustain their employment as long as they are not guilty of serious misconduct on the job. Sustaining may mean retraining for new jobs, reassignment to other areas, or creating work.

Strongly Disagree	Disagree	Neither Disagree or Agree	Agree	Strongly Agree
1	2	3	4	5

15. When a "personality" clash exists between an employee and her/his supervisor and no other jobs exist to which either party can easily be transferred, terminating the employee, not the supervisor, is an acceptable practice.

Strongly Disagree	Disagree	Neither Disagree or Agree	Agree	Strongly Agree
1	2	3	4	5

16. Employees should be allowed to use a formal grievance procedure to grieve only specific violations of established hospital policies and procedures.

Strongly Disagree	Disagree	Neither Disagree or Agree	Agree	Strongly Agree
1	2	3	4	5

17. All employees who steal prescription drugs for any reason should be terminated immediately.

Strongly Disagree	Disagree	Neither Disagree or Agree	Agree	Strongly Agree
1	2	3	4	5

18. Certain situations permit human resources managers to discuss with the boss information revealed to them in absolute confidence by an employee.

Strongly Disagree	Disagree	Neither Disagree or Agree	Agree	Strongly Agree
1	2	3	4	5

19. Distorting the truth to protect someone is an acceptable practice.

Strongly Disagree	Disagree	Neither Disagree or Agree	Agree	Strongly Agree
1	2	3	4	5

20. If the hiring salary range for a particular position is $150,000–$175,000 per year and the top candidate for the position only earns $100,000 per year, then hiring the person at $125,000 is an acceptable practice because no internal equity problems would emerge.

Strongly Disagree	Disagree	Neither Disagree or Agree	Agree	Strongly Agree
1	2	3	4	5

21. The degree of support for the annual United Way fund drive or other hospital-sponsored charity may be used as a performance criterion in appraising a manager's job performance.

Strongly Disagree	Disagree	Neither Disagree or Agree	Agree	Strongly Agree
1	2	3	4	5

22. Taking home pencils, paper clips, or other small desk items for personal use is an acceptable practice.

Strongly Disagree	Disagree	Neither Disagree or Agree	Agree	Strongly Agree
1	2	3	4	5

23. Using the office copier for personal use if the copies are of small amount is an acceptable practice.

Strongly Disagree	Disagree	Neither Disagree or Agree	Agree	Strongly Agree
1	2	3	4	5

24. Taking a "mental health day" or calling in sick after a busy period at work has ended is an acceptable practice.

Strongly Disagree	Disagree	Neither Disagree or Agree	Agree	Strongly Agree
1	2	3	4	5

25. People in general give more to an organization than they receive in return.

Strongly Disagree	Disagree	Neither Disagree or Agree	Agree	Strongly Agree
1	2	3	4	5

About the Author

CARSON F. DYE, FACHE, is a management and search consultant with Witt/Kieffer Ford Hadelman and Lloyd. He conducts chief executive officer, senior executive, and physician executive searches for various healthcare organizations. His consulting experience includes strategic planning, organizational design, and physician leadership. Also, he assists boards in executive and physician compensation, conducts board retreats, and provides counsel in chief executive officers' employment contracts and evaluation matters for a variety of client organizations. He is certified to work with the Hogan Assessment Systems tools for selection, development, and executive coaching.

Prior to entering executive search, Mr. Dye was a principal and director of Findley Davies, Inc.'s Health Care Industry Consulting Division. Prior to his consulting career, he served as chief human resources officer at St. Vincent Medical Center, Ohio

State University Medical Center, and Children's Hospital Medical Center.

Mr. Dye has been named as a physician leadership consultant expert on the LaRoche National Consultant Panel and is a member of the Governance Institute Governance One Hundred. He works with Dick Rand as a special advisor to The Healthcare Roundtable. He also serves on the faculty of the graduate program in management and health services policy at Ohio State University where he teaches both physician leadership and organizational behavior courses.

Since 1989, he has taught several programs for the American College of Healthcare Executives and he frequently speaks for state and local hospital associations. He has also authored *Leadership in Healthcare: Values at the Top* (2000) and *Protocols for Health Care Executive Behavior* (1993), both published by Health Administration Press. He has written several professional journal articles on leadership and human resources.

Mr. Dye has had a lifelong interest in leadership and its impact on organizations. He has studied how values drive leadership and how they affect change management. In addition, he studies group and organizational structure and its impact on strategy and organizational success.

Mr. Dye earned his BA from Marietta College and his MBA from Xavier University.